HOW TO PRAY WITH GOD

by

JOHN ALCOCK

How To Pray With God

ISBN: 978-164370262-9

Cover design and typesetting: Jo Marwick
Printed by CPW Printers

CONTENTS

ACKNOWLEDGEMENTS

There have been many people who have encouraged and supported me in this project and I am so grateful for their wonderful support.

Chris and Sue Willis gave me the final push to get this job done and the book into print. Their motivational encouragement and practical support has been invaluable and much appreciated.

Jo Marwick has done a magnificent job formatting and presenting the book in a professional way. I would also like to thank Jo for her patience and helpfulness and the lovely cover.

Finally, special thanks to my wife, Heather, for her patient and faithful support. Her input and encouragement were a huge help, proof reading and bringing my random ideas into a flow.

This book is written to the "whosoevers" that believe in Jesus Christ and the power of His word. I hope your life will be changed and you will be inspired to have further adventures in the Spirit with God through reading it.

Each one of us can enter the supernatural realm of God where all things are possible. Here, He is able to do beyond what we can ask, think or even imagine according to His mighty power at work in us.

Ask Him to give you the Spirit of wisdom and revelation as you read through these pages so that you can get understanding and change your world by releasing His mighty power through praying with God.

FOREWORD

When Billy Graham died, his son Franklin said he had already lost the protection of his mother's prayers and on his father's death "there is an exposure – it's like a bit of the armour is missing. So it makes me pray even harder – not only for myself, but for my family, for my children and my grandchildren".

I related to that statement, because my parents were prayer warriors too. My children grew up staying with their Grandparents on holidays and listened to their name being called out and all their uncles, aunts and cousins, as they were faithfully named and prayed for every morning.

On their death both generations, children and grandchildren asked the question "who will pray for us now"?

My wife and I decided to rise to the challenge and we committed to fill the vacuum of praying for our extended family and friends every morning.

Reading John's book and attending his Praying with God workshop has revolutionised our prayer life. As we started praying with God for our extended family, we have begun to see great change taking place - together with divine protection and purpose in our extended family, both adults and children.

I have known John and Heather for over 20 years, both in leadership of the local church and on mission trips to Mozambique, Zimbabwe and Zambia. They have remained true to their calling and this book is a practical reflection of John's dedication and faithfulness to praying with God.

I love the story of Elijah, in 1Kings 18:42, praying for rain on top of Mount Carmel, with his face between his knees It is such a beautiful picture of the teamwork between God and someone willing to pray with God. God promised rain, but Elijah had to do his part, earnestly praying for rain in order to break the drought.

I hope that in reading this book, your life is changed as much as ours has been.

Chris Willis
Creighton, July 2018

ENDORSEMENTS

In this book John shares how to pray in the Spirit in order to get answers to your prayers. The prayer model presented in this book really works! John outlines a clear step by step approach to pray effectively in and with the Holy Spirit. He calls this "Praying with God."

I have first-hand experience of using this prayer teaching both in corporate prayer meetings and when praying on my own. This model can be used to bring about both national change wherever you live, and to bring about change in your own life on a very personal level.

The key to "Praying with God" is to stir yourself up in the Holy Spirit by praying in tongues and then move on into Praying with God in the Spirit. This can be done in groups or individually.

John gives an explanation of tongues and stirring yourself to praying in the Spirit.

On a national level I have joined John and Heather and their team on prayer assignments to Wales, Israel, and Zimbabwe.

I was part of the back-up team when John Heather and team travelled to Zimbabwe.

The results of our prayers were amazing. John and Heather and the prayer team experienced many supernatural signs and wonders including healing and deliverance while they were in Israel and Zimbabwe.

In my own case I have experienced wonderful answers to prayer after Praying with God. Answers have included a new job and physical healing. I have been totally healed of Irritable Bowel syndrome, Insomnia, a skin condition on my feet and a knee condition.

Everybody who wants their prayers answered should read this book, so that they will learn the steps to "Pray with God" and have effective prayer lives.

Christine Korczak
Author and Coach
Leicester, United Kingdom

* * *

When John first explained how, why and when we should pray "With God" rather than just TO Him, it came as a huge revelation. Yes, I've declared, decreed, proclaimed, creatively interceded and agreed with the Word because I love to pray. I had never been aware that I was missing such a great key in my relationship with the LORD, until we put this teaching into practice. John's teaching is unique – it comes from a heart of humility, it's also powerful, scriptural and practically based for equipping those who want to enhance their prayer life. It opened my eyes and for me, it's become a vital part of my prayer life – I highly recommend this book.

Heather Andrew
Co-Founder: Groundbreakers
Leighton Buzzard, United Kingdom

CHAPTER ONE

INTRODUCTION

Many of us have read inspiring reports of what God has done in the past. The stories of the heroes of the faith in Heb 11 and the more modern accounts of people like Charles Finney, John G Lake, A.A. Allen or Smith Wigglesworth amongst others.

We have also heard the testimonies of the Azusa Street and Welsh revivals of the early 1900's and of the Scottish Hebrides revival and even of the more recent moves of God through people like Heidi Baker in Mozambique.

As I write this book, there are "moves" of God happening in many parts of the world.

The one thing that I see in notable past revivals is that people became deeply involved in the activity of prayer and supplication. People prayed continuously, often with travail and intercessions with moans and groaning continuing for hours, days or even weeks. The great evangelist Charles Finney credits much of his success to his intercessors Abel Clary and Daniel Nash or, Father Nash, as he is more popularly known. Nash was an American preacher who committed himself to interceding for souls. He would come quietly into towns three or four weeks before Finney's campaign began, rent a room and start to pray. Sometimes his prayerful groaning and travail would result in eviction from his room.

What is striking about reading the accounts of his prayer life is how loud and disturbing his intercessions were. Often before dawn, people could hear Father Nash from a distance of half a mile or more away praying in the woods, or praying in a church, and the sense of God's presence was overwhelming.

It is obvious that prayer and intercession plays a part in revival, but what is our part in seeing a move of God and what is God's part? Are manifestations of God's glory a sovereign move of God that happen only when He is ready? Charles Finney didn't think so. He spoke about the science of revival. He found that with the right ingredients revivals or awakenings would occur. The result of the partnership of Nash and Finney with God was dramatic, effective, life-changing and eternal.

The atmosphere over whole towns changed. People coming into towns where Father Nash had prayed, moaning and groaning in the Spirit, were convicted of their need for salvation merely by entering the locality of that town. The words preached by Charles Finney would find a very good atmosphere and fertile soil in people's hearts. The Gospel flourished with the combination of prayer and the word.

Within four months of the death of Daniel Nash, Charles Finney stopped his itinerant ministry. He knew one of the main sources of his past success was gone.

One thing to note about Charles Finney's ministry was that in the region of 80% of those who received salvation continued in Christ until they died. That is a staggering statistic. This was the result of the combination of Spirit birthed prayer and good preaching of the word. This is how I have chosen to work, because this method of praying with God has the most effective long-term impact on the lives of people who hear the gospel and are saved.

Paul the apostle also knew this and we see that he too prayed this way. He was 'in the pangs of childbirth' or travail in the Spirit for the Galatians in Gal 4:19. Note that Paul says "again" in this passage of scripture. He had birthed them first in the Spirit now he was forming them in the Spirit through his teaching and travail. He 'pastored' his people in prayer.

Many of today's pastors battle to grow their congregations both in numbers and in spiritual maturity.

It is time for the Church to travail in the Spirit again for this growth and formation of Christ in the people. Travailing prayer will produce the desired results.

Travailing prayer precedes outpourings of God's Spirit

A question many ask is why outpourings out of God's Spirit happen? Is each move of God a sovereign choice of God when He is ready, or do we the Church have something to do with it? The Bible says that we already have the same power in us that raised Jesus from the dead.

Eph 1:19. "*So that you can know and understand what is the immeasurable and unlimited and surpassing greatness of His power in and for us who believe,"*

The Bible also says that in the last days God will pour out of His Spirit upon all flesh, Acts 2:7. Note it says He will pour "out of" His Spirit, not that He will pour out His Spirit. His Spirit was poured out at Pentecost in Acts 2. Now the Spirit is within us so the rivers of the Spirit that flow, will flow from us, the Believers in Christ. John 7:38. The rivers will flow from out of our innermost beings or another way of putting it is, the rivers will be poured out of the Spirit who is within us.

So we see that the answer to the above question is that we the people of God alive today, can initiate something with Him by releasing from within our innermost beings the rivers of the mighty power of God.

He is ready and is waiting for us to work with Him.

When we the people of God start to pray **in partnership** with God the Holy Spirit, combined with the preaching of the Good News of the Gospel, we will see the atmosphere over our villages, towns and cities changed dramatically and effectively and with lasting effect.

We cannot depend on great revival leaders or "someone else" to initiate outpourings of God's Spirit for the present and for the future in our lives. We must not wait till God does something by Himself in our town. He is waiting for every one of us who are in the body of Christ today to do something where we are.

The prayer teaching and experiences with the Holy Spirit written about in this book will help empower everyone to "Pray With God" and see the Kingdom of God manifest about them.

You too can have experiences with God in your own lives where you live today!

In the middle to the late 80's in South Africa there were big political changes taking place. I was the prayer leader in a church that was very involved in prayer for the nation of South Africa at the time. The outlook was bleak. The politicians were unable to resolve the conflicts between them, war was looming and there had already been lots of bloodshed. It seemed inevitable that much more blood would be shed. Even though we met to pray earnestly, our early prayer meetings were more like political debates than prayer meetings. People would tell God what they wanted done. After one person presented their solution and request to God another person would pray something quite the opposite. I had two choices at the time: stop the corporate prayer for the nation, or get all of us to lay down our natural opinions and solutions and pray **with** God. We had to learn how to pray from a different position, the perspective of each of us being seated in Christ Jesus in heavenly places. That is how my personal journey of "Praying with God" began. We learned as a group to stir ourselves in the Spirit and to allow Him to work in and with us.

We learned how as a group to move as one as we prayed in the Spirit. We learned the rhythms and waves of the Holy Spirit as we worked with Him. God the Holy Spirit was a partner with us in our prayer work. Prayer in this group became very powerful and the unity and trust that developed among us was exceptional.

There was a miraculous outcome in South Africa. Nelson Mandela and President (at the time) De Klerk became joint winners of the Nobel Peace prize for their work in leading the country through change. There is however a story behind that story. It is the story of many of us, men and women in the Body of Christ, on our knees praying with God. It is the story of many miraculous things God did through this prayer to order events and make the changes happen the way they did. There is a book about God's divine interventions in South Africa at this time written by Dr Michael Cassidy of Africa Enterprise. (A Witness Forever – published in 1995)

Rom 8:28 in the Amplified Bible tells us that,

"All things work to the good of those who love God and are called according to His purpose God ***being a partner in their work."***

This "work" is prayer and this prayer in partnership with God always has a Godly outcome. Rom 8:26–28 are the verses in the Bible that unlocked the key to releasing the power of God through prayer for so many of us.

Another profound consequence of our intercessions at that time was that we had revival in our town, Pinetown, in the province of Kwazulu Natal. An evangelist came to our town for a week and couldn't leave. He ended up staying for six weeks and people came from many parts of South Africa to see and experience what God was doing in Pinetown.

My prayer for this **Praying With God** book is that it will show you how to pray practically and powerfully, and that it will give you some of the insight necessary to engage with God so that there will be a deeper flow of His mighty power in and through your life.

CHAPTER TWO

A NEW COVENANT FOUNDATION FOR PRAYER

In this chapter, we are going to look at establishing a foundation for effective prayer through understanding our position in the New Covenant. This is a key to praying biblical prayers and praying with God.

There is a big difference between the New Covenant and the Mosaic Covenant. These two covenants are governed by different principles. The Mosaic Covenant is based on obedience to the Law, the New Covenant is based on belief and faith in the finished work of Jesus Christ. God relates differently to His people in each of the covenants. In the Mosaic Covenant He is judge, in the New Covenant He is a Father who relates to us on the basis of what we believe and have faith for. We are no longer sinners or servants, but saints and children in a royal Kingdom. We are sons who are ambassadors, invested with power, authority and dominion. Understanding these differences will change the way we pray. **Everything** will change: our 'posture', the way we see ourselves, what we pray for, how we pray, our prayer language and the effectiveness of our prayers. So understanding the differences is a major key to praying effective prayers WITH God.

Mosaic Covenant

Under the terms of the Mosaic Covenant the core principle was obedience to the commands of God. A person's performance was continually checked against the demands of the Law which were impossible to keep. This made the people sin conscious. Prayers were therefore about asking God for mercy, for forgiveness, for deliverance from enemies, for national events. God was perceived as judge.

Psa 4: Hear me when I call, O God of my righteousness! You have relieved me in my distress;
Have mercy on me, and hear my prayer.

New Covenant

In the New Covenant the core principle is that we are in Christ, Who is Holy and Perfect. We are joined to Him and seated in Him. That makes us perfect, Heb 10:14. The book of Hebrews gives specific details about the changes and principles of the New Covenant.

Understanding our changed status and position in the New Covenant enables us to pray effectively with God.

Our New Covenant position: holy and righteous

"For by a single offering He has forever completely cleansed and perfected those who are consecrated and made holy." Heb 10:14

Many people's reaction to the above scripture is ... "Whoa! How can I be perfect, I still sin?" So why do so many Christians focus on sin? They have not embraced their new identity in Christ Jesus. They have not understood their position in the New Covenant.

Do you believe you have become the new creature the Bible says you have, or have your feelings persuaded you that nothing has really changed since you became a believer? Do you still think like this:

I still feel the same! I still think the same! I don't feel like I am a king and member of the royal family of heaven as the Bible says I am. I don't feel like I have the mighty power of God in me. I am just me!

Feelings and emotions are good, they were created by God, but they are poor masters!

A year or two ago I went on a week's narrow boat holiday on the canals of England. It was a fantastic experience but the night I came home, I lay down on my bed in my bedroom and tried to get to sleep. I felt a rocking motion and my feelings were saying to me, "You are still on the boat". Was that the truth? It felt very real! Do you think I thought, "Oh! It did not work; I obviously did not make it home. Somehow, I have remained on the boat?"

Would that have been truth because that is how I felt? The truth was I knew I was home and said to my feelings, "I am at home in my bed and that is where I am going to stay and sleep." When I woke up, guess what? My feelings had changed and fallen in line with the truth that I was at home and so the room was steady.

Why do I tell this story? **Because truth received is truth whether you feel it or not.** If you allow your thoughts to conform to the truth of God's word and choose to hold onto and believe God's word, your feelings will come in line with that truth as my feelings did in the narrow boat experience.

So don't focus on your feelings, focus on thinking God's Word and then your feelings will fall in line with your thoughts and not the other way around. We don't want our feelings to shape our lives and world view. Choosing to think about and believe who we are in this New Covenant will change the way we pray.

Believing you are a new man is a choice.

Do you believe that what the Lord says in His word about who you now are is true and real, or not?

Believing is a choice. You do not need faith to believe, you **choose** to believe and then God gives you faith as you act on His truth that you have chosen to believe.

Faith comes by hearing and hearing by the Word of God. If you do not choose to believe God's Word you will not hear it!

So back to what God says has happened to you when you received Christ.

Choose right now to believe what He says about you!

You are not just 'human' when you become born again. You have become a new creature. You are spirit. Your heavenly Father is Spirit. Your new identity is spirit. You are one spirit with Christ. That part of you is perfect already. But even though you are spirit, you have a soul and live in your body while on the earth. Your spirit is perfect, your soulish area, that is your mind and emotions are being transformed continually if you keep renewing your mind by the word of God (Rom 12:2). Your mind and emotions are the part of you that need the work.

Your mind and emotions are being changed by the word of God. The study of the word of God combined with your choice to believe the word of God transforms you into the image of Christ. Your past behaviour before you were born again is changing. Your desires are changing. Your value system is changing as you continue to choose daily to believe the word. It is the side of you that Jesus Christ as the Author and Finisher of your faith is working in.

Paul says it this way in Eph 4:22–24.

"Strip yourselves of your former nature (put off and discard your old unrenewed self) which characterised your previous manner of life and becomes corrupt through lusts and desires that spring from delusion. And be constantly renewed in the spirit of your mind (having a fresh mental and spiritual attitude) And put on the new nature (the regenerate self) created in God's image, (Godlike) in true righteousness and holiness." Amplified Bible.

If you sin you don't become a sinner. You are a righteous person who needs to repent. You are still the righteousness of God in Christ Jesus. That status of righteousness is a permanent gift to you from God and does not depend on your performance.

You received the gift of righteousness by believing in Christ, you keep it by believing in Christ.

As you choose to believe the word of God and what has happened to you, you learn of His goodness and kindness to you. This understanding of that goodness and kindness produces change in you.

It is the grace of God that leads us to repentance. Titus 2:11–12.

"For the grace of God has come forward for the deliverance from sin and the eternal salvation for all mankind. It has trained us to reject all ungodliness and worldly desires, to live discreet upright devout lives in this present world." Amplified Bible.

Your Body is the temple of the Holy Spirit

The third part of you, your body, is the temple of the Holy Spirit. 1 Cor 6:19.

Your body is quickened by the power of the Spirit. Rom 8:11.

"And if the Spirit of Him Who raised up Jesus from the dead dwells in you, then He Who raised up Christ Jesus from the dead will also restore to life

your mortal short-lived perishable bodies through His Spirit Who dwells in you." Amplified Bible.

So we work out our salvation to complete the process in our soul and emotions through study of the word, fellowship with the Holy Spirit and prayer. Phil 2:12.

Our new Covenant Position: Justified

Another aspect of your New Covenant position is that we are justified. Fully grasping this will also change the way we pray.

Let me explain now what being justified and declared righteous means to born again believers in Christ.

Rom 5:1. *"Therefore since we are justified (acquitted, declared righteous, and given a right standing with God) through faith, let us grasp the fact that we have the peace of reconciliation to hold and to enjoy peace with God through our Lord Jesus Christ the Messiah, the Anointed One."*

Strong's (*dikaioō* G1344) translates the word justified as: *to show, exhibit, evince, one to be righteous, such as he is and wishes himself to be considered. To declare, pronounce, one to be just, righteous, or such as he ought to be.*

Every born again Christian believer has been declared righteous (justified) by God the great judge, and given a status of grace and favour with Him. This is through their faith.

How can God who is a good judge, declare us believers in the Lord Jesus Christ righteous, not guilty, innocent of our failings and unrighteous acts?

If someone went to court and was proven guilty during the course of their trial, the judge would have to impose a sentence that the guidelines of the law required.

If the judge made up his own sentence or said something like, "I am in a good mood today and I find the defendant really funny so I am acquitting him even though he is guilty and justice demands that he is punished." That judge would not be a good judge and would be disbarred.

The judge has to weigh up the facts, with his or her expert knowledge of the law, make an appropriate judgement, and then sentence accordingly.

Now the Great Judge, God, has declared that the wages of sin is death. So how can He declare now you are innocent? Many Christians will say, "He has forgiven us through the sacrifice of Jesus on the cross." Or they will say, "The blood of Jesus has washed my sin away." Both these statements are true but they do not carry the full impact of what has caused God to declare us righteous. If that was the full basis for our salvation, as many believe, we will not have not been sentenced and our consciences would still condemn us.

God would still know I did things I wasn't punished for, I would know I did bad things and be glad He has forgiven me. Yet, I would still carry the shame and regret and sorrow of my past and even embarrassment in God's presence because, He knows all about me! What I am really like.

I could keep getting flashbacks to horrible things I had done in the past and could be motivated by guilt as I lived my new life in Christ. My conscience could really spoil things.

Let me tell you a parable here to bring more of God's truth to deal with our problem with our conscience.

A man brutally assaulted and raped a woman in his home. She laid charges and he was arrested and brought to trial. The whole town was talking about this case. The court was packed on the day of sentencing. The judge had found the man guilty of the charges. As he is about to pass sentence the woman victim stands up and says, "Sir, I would like to withdraw all charges. I have chosen to forgive the man. He has said he is sorry."

The judge then bangs down his gavel and says, "Case dismissed, the prisoner is free to go."

Everyone would be talking about how lucky the man was to be free even though he is such a brute and guilty. He would be shunned. The man himself would carry the shame and consequences of his actions for the rest of his life.

This is the state of many Christians. They know they are forgiven, but they are still trapped by the weight of their past. They carry guilt and shame. They think there is always someone around them who is a better Christian than they are.

Now let us go back to that courtroom at the time of judgement and consider a different scenario.

As the judge considers the facts, he says, "I have just been given new evidence. This man looks the same as the man who did this, he even lives in the same house but he is not the same man. The man who did this evil deed is in fact dead. This is not the same man. You are acquitted of all charges as you are innocent! You may leave the court."

There would be a surge of approval through the courtroom. Justice has been done. People would flock around the defendant and tell him how glad they are this is over and that he has been exonerated and his name cleared. The judge would be commended for seeing justice has been done and that he has declared the man righteous and innocent of all charges.

The man would know that he is innocent and would not carry any guilt or regret into his future. People in his community would know he was innocent and not talk about him. He would get on with his life with no shame, guilt or regret.

Now let us see what this means to you and I, the New Covenant believer in Jesus Christ.

All of us were sinners. Gone astray. Trapped in our sin and iniquities. Even good people fall short of God's standard of perfection. And then, by the grace of God and the drawing of the Holy Spirit we come to Christ. We receive Jesus, believe in our hearts and confess with our mouths, "He is Lord." We call upon His name and decide to follow Him.

Now let us look at what actually happens legally to allow the Great Judge, our Father, at this point to declare us righteous.

Rom 6:3–7. *"Are you ignorant of the fact that all of us who have been baptised into Christ Jesus were baptised into His death? We were buried with Him by the baptism into death, so that just as Christ was raised from the dead, so we too might live and behave in newness of life. For if we have become one with Him by sharing a death like His, we shall also be one with him by sharing His resurrection by a new life lived for God."*

"We know that our old unrenewed self was nailed to the cross with Him that our body, which is the instrument of sin, might be made ineffective and inactive for evil that we may no longer be slaves of sin. For when a man dies he is freed from the power of sin. If we have died with Christ we shall also live with him."

Remember the wages of sin is death. Well, God the Great Judge has seen this law obeyed to the full. **We sinned and therefore we died. How? In Christ Jesus on the cross!**

God sees us to be in Christ Jesus. 1 Cor 6:17 tells us that: *"the person who is united to the Lord is one Spirit with Him."* If you join yourself to Christ you are one spirit with Him.

2 Cor 5:14. *"The love of Christ compels us that if One died for all, then all died."*

Just as in the parable I shared, the one who did the crime died and the one who was charged was not that man, but was innocent of all charges, so you are not the person who has done all the bad stuff. That person has been crucified in Christ Jesus on the cross and has died. You are a new creature, in the same house, your body. You look like that person and even feel like that person but you are not that person. The old you is dead!

Paul says it like this in Gal 2:20

"I have been crucified with Christ, it is no longer I who live but Christ lives in me and the life which I now live in the flesh I live by faith in the Son of God who loved me and gave Himself up for me."

The New Testament believer has been crucified in Christ and raised to new life. He or she is a brand new creature 2 Cor 5:17. The old spiritual and moral condition has passed away. Behold the fresh and new has come. We are not that old man or woman! Choose to believe this. Every time the voice of the accuser comes to remind you of things your old self did in the past, you say out loud, "That person is dead, I am not that person! I am a new creation in Christ Jesus."

Our New Covenant Position: We are in union with and joined to Christ.

In the New Covenant, we are in union with and joined to Christ, the One who fulfilled the old covenant and the Law, and Who is perfect. There is no longer a wall between God and us because we are in Him and we are seated in Him in the heavenly realm. (Eph 2:6).

Remember what Jesus said to Saul in Acts 9:4, *"Saul, Saul. Why are you persecuting Me?"*

Saul was persecuting the church at the time and had plans to persecute even more of the believers in Christ.

How could Saul persecute Jesus? Jesus was already in heaven. Why would Jesus say, "Why are you persecuting Me?" Because born again believers are one with and in Him.

See 1 Cor 6:17. *"The person who is united to the Lord becomes one spirit with Him."*

The Lord Jesus Christ also thinks we are one with Him, so close in fact, He said that He personally was being persecuted. Do you see that? We are in Him.

What happens if you step out to do something for the Father? Christ steps out with you to do something for the Father because you are in Him and He's in you. How do we know what the Father wants us to do? We read His Word. The Word tells us clearly in most cases what to do.

You are a new spiritual creation. You must come boldly to the throne of grace to ask for help if you need help. See Heb 4:16. He will freely and lovingly give you the help you need to overcome your temptations and challenges.

Come as the beloved "son" you are and not as a miserable unworthy sinner.

You are a king and a priest to God. Rev 1:5–6. You are part of Him and in Him who is on the throne in heaven.

2 Cor 5:17 *"Therefore if any person is engrafted in Christ the Messiah he is a new creation, a new creature altogether, the old previous moral and spiritual condition has passed away. Behold the fresh and new has come."*

Note the word engrafted in the above scripture. Engrafted means 'to be joined to.'

Note also that the old life has passed away and everything is fresh and new.

To be confident and bold in our union and partnership with Christ, it is very important that we understand that we really are in Christ.

Understanding the difference in the way the Father considers and views New Covenant believers in Christ, is the foundation of earth shaking effective prayer and will enable us to flow very easily and comfortably with the Holy Spirit. We must not be sin conscious, and focused on our personal feelings and failings which is Old Covenant behaviour, but must know that His glory and power are in us. We must approach and address God with boldness. Our status and position in the New Covenant give us this right. We are holy and righteous, we are justified, we are new creatures.

We are not praying to the Father from a distant place, but we are literally seated in Christ Whom we are joined to. We are able to offer worthy and relevant prayer to an awesome God who hears us and loves us.

We are New Covenant Intercessors

It is time to deal with another thing we hear in the church today. "Intercessors must stand in the gap and must repent of the sins of the people. They must take on the weight of those sins or identify with them fully and then ask God to have mercy on them on behalf of those places or people."

This thinking is based on the Mosaic Covenant and is an Old Covenant type prayer. Moses and Daniel did that. In the Old Covenant, intercessors stood in the gap between man and God and pleaded on the behalf of men before God. Now in the New Covenant we are seated in Christ Jesus in heavenly places. So must we get out of Christ to stand before Him in the gap? The answer is clearly no. The truth of the matter is that we the New Covenant intercessors are a part of the intercession ministry of the Lord Jesus Christ. We work in this ministry with the Lord Jesus in the Holy Spirit. We work in partnership with God.

In Heb 7:35 and Rom 8:34 we read that Jesus intercedes for us and in Rom 8:27 that the Holy Spirit also intercedes for us. In Eph 6:18, Paul tells us to pray in the Spirit with all manner of prayer and entreaty and to intercede for all the saints. He does the same again in 1 Tim 2:1–8. This is all one and the same ministry. The intercession ministry of the Lord Jesus.

At Calvary the Lord Jesus Christ took the sins of this world onto Himself once for all time. He will never do that again. Now we New Covenant believers are in Him. What we do, He does. What He does, we do. Are we going to try to put Christ under a burden of sin again? Never! I certainly will not do this. I will stay hid in Christ and do His ministry in the Holy Spirit.

Jesus called the Holy Spirit, Intercessor, in John 16:7. In the Strong's Concordance we see what Jesus called this One He was sending to be with us. "Comforter, Counselor, Strengthener, Helper, Advocate, Intercessor, Standby."

Jesus also called Him the Spirit of Truth in John 16:13. I will work with what He gives me to work with and no more. I will pray with Him as He shows and leads me. This is what I see a son of God doing in a case where there is manifest ungodliness in a place. This is New Covenant prayer, not standing in the gap, but from a place of being seated in and joined to Him. The Holy Spirit is also called Advocate. He knows exactly how to present prayers of intercession on the basis of the shed blood of Jesus and pray on behalf of God's people in accordance with the perfect will of God.

Therefore we need to pray in the Spirit with all manner of prayer and entreaty at all times as Paul commands us to in Eph 6:18.

CHAPTER THREE

WHY DO WE NEED TO PRAY?

Many Christians believe in what I call a "que sera sera" mentality, "whatever's to be will be."

In other words, whatever God wants to happen will happen anyway, without any involvement from us. This is fatalistic and ungodly thinking. We need to get out of this mentality and see that we can and need to control our destiny through prayer. God has given us the keys to His kingdom and we need to use these keys. If we were given the keys to a motor car and we never used these keys when we got into that motor car, we would get nowhere. The same is true in exercising our given authority in the spirit realm. We need to use the keys we have been given to move forward in our call in this life (Eph 2:10) and to advance the things of God's kingdom around us.

You have not because you ask not.

Jesus is our first example of the need to pray. He only did what the Father wanted Him to do, and He only spoke what the Father gave Him to speak. If the Father was going to say and do what He had already decided to say and do, then why did Jesus have to pray? Heb 5:7.

"In the days of His flesh Jesus offered up definite, special petitions for that which He not only wanted but needed and supplications with strong

crying and tears to Him who was always able to save Him out from death, and He was heard because of His reverence toward God, His piety, in that He shrank from the horrors of separation from the bright presence of the Father."

Jesus knew the principles of the Kingdom. Even though He was so in touch with and connected to the Father, He still prayed what He saw the Father doing into existence. He asked the Father for whatever the Father wanted to do.

In John 11:22 Martha says to Jesus, *"I know that whatever You ask from the Father, He will grant You."* She had seen Jesus asking the Father for things in prayer. Jesus did not correct her, because she was right. Whatever He asked the Father for in prayer would be granted Him.

In John 11:41 Jesus lifts up His eyes and says, "Father I thank You that You have heard Me." He had already prayed to the Father for Lazarus's resurrection.

This same principle applies to us who are in Christ. We can also ask the Father for anything if we abide in Him John 15:7,

"If you live in Me, abide vitally united to Me and My words remain in you and continue to live in your hearts, ask whatever you will and it will be done for you."

At the end of James 4:2, the apostle says, "You do not have because you do not ask."

In the first epistle of John chapter 5 in verses 14–15 this is reinforced,

"And this is the confidence we have in Him, we are sure that if we ask anything according to His will, He listens to and hears us."

What is the will of the Father? It is that we abide in the word and make our requests to Him in the name of Jesus. John 16:23–24 and verses 26–27. If we ask in the name of Jesus, He hears us because as we use the name of Jesus, we are representing Jesus Himself. It is as if Jesus Himself is asking the Father.

John 5:14 *"And since we know that He listens to us in whatever we ask, we also know with settled and absolute knowledge that we have granted us as our present possessions the requests made of Him."*

Prayer establishes the will of God

The first example is in Exod 17:8–13. Israel were travelling through the wilderness to the Promised Land and were attacked by the Amalekites. Moses went up on a hill with the rod of God and Joshua engaged the enemy in the valley below. When Moses held up his arms, Israel triumphed. When he lowered his arms, the Amalekites started winning. We see this in verse 11. So, Aaron and Hur supported his arms, one on each side of Moses, and Israel won the day.

There are significant lessons to be learned from this account. It was God's will that Israel possessed the Promised Land. It was not His will for Israel to be defeated by the Amalekites. What would have happened if Moses had sat there thinking, "I'm tired! Let Joshua and the army fight this battle. I'll watch!"

I think it is clear that Israel would have been defeated. The Bible would have ended there. Was that God's will? No, it was not! Moses's intervention made the difference. It released the power and authority of God into the situation which strengthened Israel and enabled them to win the battle.

In Eph 6:10 Paul tells us to be strong in the Lord and in His mighty power. Why does he do this? So that we will prevail in our battles. It is not God's will that we lose the battles we fight, and then live in defeat. Just as God did not fight the battle against the Amalekites for Israel, but strengthened them in the battle, God will not fight your battles without you, but will strengthen and be with you in your battles.

Now let's look at 1 Tim 2:1–8. I will quote verse 8.

"I desire therefore that in every place men should pray, without quarrelling or resentment or doubt in their minds, lifting up holy hands."

Moses was doing that on the hill, he was holding up holy hands.

Why should we pray lifting holy hands? Let us look at 1 Tim 2:3–4,

"For such praying is good and right, and it is pleasing and acceptable to God our Saviour, Who wishes all men to be saved and increasingly to perceive and recognise and discern and know precisely the divine Truth." (Amplified Bible).

Are all people been saved right now? The answer is no! God's will is clearly not happening then in this case. So what are we to do about this? Shrug our shoulders and think, "When God is ready, in time to come, there is going to be a big revival and then multitudes of people will get saved." Charles Finney and Daniel Nash did not think like that. Moses on the hill and Paul the apostle did not think like that, and nor should we. Paul commands this type of praying because the will of the Father is "that all men be saved." This type of prayer pleases God because it is effective as it creates an atmosphere, as did the prayers of Daniel Nash and others, for the Gospel to flourish.

So prayer that God is pleased with is the prayers we are told to pray in 1 Tim 2:1–2

"First of all then, I admonish and urge that petitions, prayers, intercessions and thanksgivings be offered on behalf of all men.

For kings and all who are in positions of authority or high responsibility, that outwardly we may pass a quiet and undisturbed life and inwardly a peaceable one in all godliness and reverence and seriousness in every way."

So if we make prayers and intercessions for all men as we are instructed to do by Paul, we will see many more getting saved. We will also see Christ formed in those who are already saved. Isn't this exactly what Daniel Nash and Charles Finney were doing? Yes! And it is also exactly what Jesus is doing right now as it is described in Heb 7:25. We will talk about how Jesus does this later in the book in the section about the intercession prayer of Jesus.

Prayer releases tremendous power from the throne room

"The earnest heartfelt continued prayer of a righteous man makes tremendous power available dynamic in its working." James 5:16 Amplified Bible.

It is this kind of prayer that releases power that changes things and brings us the victory in our battles.

Let us look at an example of where this power was released. In Acts 16 we read about Paul and Silas doing the work of the ministry and then getting into trouble when Paul casts a spirit of divination out of a slave girl who was following them around. As a result of this, they ended up being attacked and then thrown into jail. This is what happened next in the jail. Acts 16:25,

"But about midnight, as Paul and Silas were praying and singing hymns of praise to God, and the other prisoners were listening to them,

Suddenly there was a great earthquake, so that the very foundations of the prison were shaken; and at once all the doors opened and everyone's shackles were unfastened." (Amplified Bible).

These two men had been doing the work of God when these unfortunate things happened to them. Notice they did not sit in their stocks and ask God why He allowed this to happen to them, and tell God how they didn't deserve this. They prayed and praised God with thanksgiving.

Are you in a bad place right now, whether it is as a result of your own actions or the actions of others? Do you need a release of power? Do what Paul and Silas did. Pray and worship God with thanksgiving.

Let us look at what happened from God's point of view in heaven as to why the jail Paul and Silas were praying and worshipping in got shaken. Rev 5:8.

"And when He had taken the scroll, the four living creatures and the twenty-four elders of the heavenly Sanhedrin prostrated themselves before the Lamb. Each was holding a harp (lute or guitar), and they had bowls full of incense (fragrant spices or gums for burning), which are the prayers of God's people the saints."

See how precious our prayers are. They are contained in golden bowls before the very throne of God. Now let us see what happens to the prayers of the saints, bearing in mind that power is released through the prayers of a righteous man, according to James 5:16. Turning to Rev 8:5,

"So the angel took the censer and filled it with fire from the altar and cast it upon the earth. Then there followed peals of thunder and loud rumblings and blasts and noises, and flashes of lightning and an earthquake."

Paul and Silas released the incense of prayer and thanksgiving. The angel in heaven before the throne of God collected this incense and then filled the censer with fire from the altar and cast it down upon the jail. The result was astounding. The jail was shaken to pieces by an earthquake and the shackles of every person in that jail fell off. Yet, they did not run away. There was a glory released in the jail, that was so appealing and so beautiful, that even hardened criminals were touched by it.

The jailer knew what these criminals were like because he worked with them the whole time. He was going to kill himself because he was certain everyone had run away. This was obviously something very different and out of the ordinary. They were all still there. He and his family were immediately saved.

This is also what happened to the atmosphere in towns where Daniel Nash prayed. There was a glory released that was so beautiful and so appealing that multitudes were drawn to Christ.

A little while ago there was TV footage of the aftermath of the earthquake in Haiti. There were pictures of a jail in one of the town centres where the wall of the jail had collapsed. The jail was empty, not a soul in sight. I immediately thought of what had happened with Paul and Silas when I saw that footage. The glory presence of God in the Philippian jail must have been awesome because in that earthquake nobody ran away.

There are more accounts in the Bible of the release of this earthquake and lightning power from the throne room of God as a result of prayer:

In Acts 4:31 prayer is being offered to God by the disciples. Once again incense is being collected before the throne of God. Picture the scene in heaven as the angel dips the censer into the fire on the altar and throws it down on the room where the apostles are praying. The whole room shakes and the Glory of God fills the room.

In Acts 12:5 we see the church praying for Peter who is also in jail. In verse 7 again we see shackles fall off and the prison door or gate is opened.

God is not a respecter of persons. These same things happen for us today.

A few years ago before the change of government in South Africa, the son of a friend of our family, who was interested in photography, went to Zambia. He was arrested there, because of the photographic equipment he was carrying, and was accused of being a spy for the apartheid government.

Things looked really bad for him. South African government officials were trying to get him back but nothing was working. I got down to praying in the Holy Spirit for him. After about two hours or so of prayer, I suddenly had a release. I knew he was coming home. I told my mother to tell his parents their son was coming home. They said thank you when they got the message but were not really that confident in my news. Miraculously, the prison doors were opened and within a week he was home. The official reason was that he had been pardoned by the President. The real reason was that fire fell from the altar of God onto that jail.

Here is another case of a power intervention from the throne room. Psa 18:3–19. I won't quote this whole passage of scripture because it is very long. Briefly, David is in trouble and calls out to God for help. This is what verse 7 says,

"Then the earth quaked and rocked, the foundations also of the mountains trembled; they were moved and were shaken because He was indignant and angry."

Verse 13, *"The Lord also thundered from the heavens, and the Most high uttered His voice, amidst hailstones and coals of fire."*

There was a discharge of power from the throne of God, in the manner we have being looking at.

David also knew about the release of the power of God through the incense of prayer. We see this in Psa 141:2,

"Let my prayer be set forth as incense before You, the lifting of my hands as the evening sacrifice."

You can read about the same kind of release of God's power from the throne room in a thunder being released against the Phillistines in 1 Sam 7:10.

Here are further reasons to pray.

1. Prayer is a command, we are told to pray. Tim 2 1:8. Eph 6:18.
2. It releases God's peace to guard our hearts and minds. Phil 4:6–7.
3. It brings revelation and understanding Eph 1:17–19.
4. Words are given to preach. Eph 6:19.
5. Prayer causes Christ to be formed in us. Gal 4:19.
6. Prayer gives us courage Eph 6:19
7. Prayer causes the peace of God to garrison about us. Phil 4:6–7.
8. It opens doors of opportunity Col 4:3–4
9. Prayer causes us to be strengthened Eph 3:16
10. Prayer causes the mighty power of God in us to take us beyond what we can ask or even imagine Eph 3:20.
11. It gives strength and endurance Col 1:11.

To conclude, the prayers and intercessions of the righteous are critical for things to change. Your prayer and my prayer achieve the same result before God as the prayers of Paul the apostle, David, Moses, Samuel and Jesus Himself.

Prayer changes us and circumstances. It brings us into God's realm and puts us in a place of communion with Him. It takes us out of the natural realm into the unseen realm.

So let us get on with it, we have mighty weapons and do not need to feel helpless. Be encouraged and strengthened in you walk with God. Our prayers are vital and tremendously effective.

CHAPTER FOUR

PARTNERING WITH GOD

A powerful principle for effective prayer is praying in partnership **with** God. This means praying with God and not to Him. We can and must pray with God! There is power that is unleashed through prayer with God that changes situations, events, people and even nations.

Let me give you an example of this in the Bible. It is the story of God and Elijah working together. James 5:16 says that

"the heartfelt continued prayer of a righteous man makes dynamic power available."

This is effectual prayer. It is prayer that works. It is prayer that releases the power of God. This is how Elijah prayed as he worked with God.

In James 5:17–18 we are told how Elijah prayed earnestly for it not to rain, and so no rain fell on the earth for three and a half years, and then how he prayed again for it to rain, and the heavens supplied rain again.

How could Elijah pray with such power that it did not rain for so long, and then pray again that the rain would come, and it did!

We will see that **it was because there was a partnership between him and God**. In 1 Kings 18:1 God says,

"Go show yourself to Ahab and I will send rain on the earth."

God wanted to send the rain. It was God's plan and idea. So Elijah partnered with God to accomplish this. In 1 Kings 18:42 Elijah goes up Mount Carmel to pray. In 1 Kings 18:44 the result of the prayer was manifest in a cloud the size of a man's fist over the sea. God's plan was accomplished. Note how James the apostle says that what happened to the weather happened because of Elijah's prayers and not because God said, "I am sending rain." God needed Elijah to work with Him to accomplish His plan and James says the the reason for the successful result was due to Elijah's prayers.

What's the point of ineffectual prayer? Nothing! Let us pray effectively not beating the air! We ensure we pray effectively by praying with God, in union with Him, in partnership with Him.

Is it possible that there are things that the Father wants to do today in our lives, in our towns and in our cities that He cannot do until we partner with Him? How many prophetic words and promises of God are still waiting to be prayed into life with the Holy Spirit? Someone needs to put their head between their knees as Elijah did on Mount Carmel and travail these promises and plans of God into manifestation.

One of the worst things we as Christians can think is, "Well, God is sovereign so what He wants to do He will do. I am only human I can't change things so I will tell Him about all the problems I see and just trust Him to sort things out."

This way of thinking is unscriptural. God wants to work through and with us. There is plenty we can do. We are not merely powerless human beings. We are new creatures in Christ full of His power and authority. We can move mountains!

What would have happened if when God told Elijah, "I am sending the rain," Elijah had simply said, "Lord God, I know You are powerful and omnipotent so I will watch you bring the rain if that is your will." If it was his prayer that brought the rain as James says it was, what would have happened if Elijah had thought that God is able to do what He wants to do by Himself, and so done nothing?

I think it is clear! **Nothing would have happened!** We have to know who we are in Christ and how our Father works through and with us in the earth today for this very reason! Let us be those people who partner and work with God and see His mighty power unleashed to accomplish His plans today.

Therefore, it is essential that we engage in prayer in which we partner with God.

Praying in tongues in partnership with the Holy Spirit.

One of the names that Jesus calls the Holy Spirit who is to come is Intercessor. (John 16:7 Amplified Bible). He is the One who knows all things. We need to get to know Him as such and move into a prayer ministry with Him.

We do this by praying in tongues and moving into intercession with Him as He works in and with us.

Many years ago when I was a less experienced prayer leader, I had one of the lead intercessors from Youth With A Mission come to one of my prayer meetings. In this prayer meeting we prayed mainly in tongues in the Holy Spirit. As I was taking him back to where he was staying, I realised with a shock he was not pleased with how we had prayed.

"But you didn't pray the Word in your prayer meeting. You have to pray the Word when you pray!"

Have you ever heard that comment? I was shaken by this as I was still learning the art of prayer myself. But God wasn't shocked at this and gave me the revelation I did not have at that time. The following understanding helped me.

If someone prays in a prayer meeting in a language you do not understand, does that mean their prayer is a waste of time? What happens if that person is an international prayer leader from another nation with an amazing track record in answered prayer whose language you do not understand?

You would not think his prayers in your prayer meeting were a waste of time.

You would let him pray and then ask someone to interpret. Do you think the devil would not understand his language if he didn't pray in English or whatever language you speak.

Well! The Holy Spirit is the best prayer leader anywhere in existence. He comes to your prayer meetings. You are very privileged! He prays in your prayer meetings through you. He prays in a spiritual language different to your natural language. Do these prayers carry weight? Is the devil effected by the power unleashed through them? Are these prayers worth something? Yes! Yes! Yes!

Is the Holy Spirit in submission to the scriptures. Yes! Psa 138:2 tells us God has put the word even above His name. Is the Holy Spirit God? Yes!

Look at Eph 6:17,

"And take the helmet of salvation and the sword which the Spirit wields which is the Word of God."

There it is in the Word very clearly. The Holy Spirit wields the Word of God! This is both in the words He gives you to speak in your spiritual language, and the word of God He gives you to decree in your understanding.

Declaring Forgiveness with God the Holy Spirit

The gospel of Jesus Christ is good news. There is an incorrect perception and understanding that God is angry with the sin of the world and it's under the judgement and wrath of God. The scripture clearly shows that there will be a time for this. At present however, God is extending an appeal to the world through the gospel to be reconciled to Him. The word tells us that, *"God so loved the world that He gave up His only begotten Son, so that whoever believes in Him should not perish but have eternal life."* John3:16

1 Tim 2:4, *"Who wishes all men to be saved and increasingly to perceive and recognise and discern and know precisely and correctly the divine truth."*

We as New Covenant intercessors in Christ Jesus do not need to be pleading for mercy from God. He has already shown His mercy to the whole world in the crucifixion of Jesus Christ.

2 Cor 5:19 says, *"It was God personally present in Christ, reconciling and restoring the world to favour with Himself, not counting up and holding against men their trespasses but cancelling them and committing to us the message of reconciliation of the restoration to favour."* Amplified Bible.

We New Testament believers are Christ's ambassadors, and our job is to make an appeal to people to receive this favour and mercy of God, that is now offered, and for them to be reconciled to God.

If people, regions, cities and nations are blinded to the good news and favour that God has made available to them they cannot receive what He has offered. Normally what causes this blinded state is that these people, cities or regions are given over to demonic activity and control.

In the sinful state they are in, they are blinded by demonic forces. 2 Cor 4:4 says,

"For the god of this world has blinded the unbelievers minds that they should not discern the truth, preventing them from seeing the illuminating light of the Gospel of the Glory of Christ the Messiah, Who is the Image and Likeness of God."

So as ambassadors of Christ we can declare and release God's forgiveness and blessing to the people in places we go to, through the ministry of the Holy Spirit. The gospel is good news. We want people blessed by the good news. We want their minds clear and open to understand the Gospel. By decreeing the mercy and grace of God released to a place that has manifest sinfulness, we can attack the powers and principalities who are behind the observed behaviour of the people of that place and get those people free to hear and understand the Gospel. The forgiveness of God breaks the connection between demonic powers and the people. It takes away the legal right of these powers and principalities to operate in that place. This brings down the confidence of these powers to oppose the message of Christ. They have already been disarmed through the cross of Jesus Christ, (Col 2:15), so we can push them out the way by a combination of prayer in the Spirit and by the preaching of the word of God . The cross was the place of sacrifice of Jesus Christ that took away the sins of the world. This is the source of the forgiveness. That is the very thing we enforce against the rulers of darkness because it is the thing that has disarmed them. We can then invade that place with the preaching and demonstration of the Kingdom.

Prov 21:22, *"A wise man scales the city walls of the mighty and brings down the stronghold in which they trust."*

This is a bit like the walls of Jericho being brought down. Once the walls at Jericho fell the battle was virtually over. Israel charged into the city and took it. Likewise, when we bless and declare the forgiveness from sin of the people in a place, we bring down the stronghold in which the demonic rulers of that place trust, and we open the way for the Kingdom of God to be released in that place.

John 20:23, *"Now having received the Holy Spirit and being led and directed by Him, if you forgive the sins of anyone, they are forgiven; if you retain the sins of anyone, they are retained." (Amplified Bible).*

Paul also comments on forgiving in 2 Cor 2:10–11,

"If you forgive anyone anything, I too forgive that one; and what I have forgiven; if I have forgiven anything, has been for your sakes in the presence of and with the approval of Christ the Messiah, to keep Satan from getting the advantage over us; for we are not ignorant of his wiles and intentions."

We can do this for one person or many people, the principle is the same.

The Holy Spirit does this with us because the Lamb of God came to take away the sins of the world. As an ambassador of Christ this is acting in accordance with the will of the Father and Jesus who are in heaven. The Holy Spirit would never be involved in anything against the Father's will anyway. The fact is the sins of these people or places are already forgiven. They have not appropriated this forgiveness by receiving Christ because they have not heard and understood the good news of the gospel.

So in a sin situation we can release the forgiveness of God and bless a person, or group of people, or a place like a city or town. We do this praying in the Holy Spirit because He the Advocate, will present their case perfectly before the throne of God based on the shed blood of Jesus at Calvary and then we decree what He gives us to decree. Look at 1 Cor 14:16,

"Otherwise if you ***bless*** *and render thanks with your spirit thoroughly aroused by the Holy Spirit"*

The Holy Spirit blesses as you pray in your prayer language.

Blessing people is speaking and releasing the goodness of God to them. The goodness of God in this case is that there is mercy and grace freely extended to them.

Who wouldn't want to partner with God the Holy Spirit in prayer? The benefits of praying with God are very effective. You are secure in Him and you will never take on something you cannot deal with if you work with Him. Eph 6:10 is a command,

"Finally my brethren be strong in the Lord and in the power of His might."

When we pray with God, joined to Him, we can be fearless in our prayer. We will succeed in every prayer assignment whatever it is. His power and ability will be released in every one of these situations. We can do all things through Christ Who strengthens us.

Why pray without knowing all the facts and the will of God for any situation. By partnering with the Holy Spirit we can get involved with the prayer ministry of God Himself in and for that situation in perfect harmony and agreement with His will. He is the One that knows how to make it all work out for good.

Rom 8:28: *"We are assured and know that God being a partner in their labour all things work together and are fitting into a plan for good to and for those who love Him and are called according to His design and purpose."*

CHAPTER FIVE

DIFFERENT TYPES OF PRAYERS

As we partner with God in prayer we must allow Him to guide and direct us in the type of prayer He wants to pray in and for a particular situation. As we learn the prayer patterns and rhythms of the Holy Spirit we will start to recognise some of the types of prayer He is praying with and through us. We will also recognise when He is changing the prayer and moving it into a different type of prayer. We will examine some of the prayer types in this chapter.

Eph 6:18–19, "Pray at all times on every occasion ***in the Spirit with all manner of prayer*** *and entreaty. To that end keep alert and watch with strong purpose and perseverance, interceding in behalf of all the saints God's consecrated people. And pray also for me that freedom of utterance is given me that I may open my mouth to boldly proclaim the mystery of the Good News the Gospel."*

The Aramaic Bible in Plain English puts it this way,

"Pray with ***all prayers*** *and with all desires always* ***in The Spirit****."*

And the International Standard Version says,

"Pray ***in the Spirit*** *at all times with* ***every kind of prayer and request****."*

The different translations clearly convey the idea that there are different types of prayers and that they must be prayed in the Spirit.

Different Types of Prayer have different Rules

The reference to 'all manner of prayers' indicates that there are many types of prayers. Some of these are travail, petitions, intercessions, thanksgiving, blessing, warfare, praise and declaration. Each one has different rules.

The following example has been used by other Bible teachers but it is so good, I will use it here.

Imagine I was to say to a room full of people, "Let's play ball!" There might be some confusion as each person thinks of a different ball game. Each would visualise their favourite ball game: rugby, or tennis, or polo or hockey and so on. Each game has a unique instrument, environment and a specific set of rules. The type of ball is different. The rules for rugby do not apply or work for a game of tennis.

It is the same for prayer. Each type of prayer has unique principles.

There are already many books, websites and blogs devoted to the different types of prayers so we will just select a few as examples.

Prayers of Petition

Petition prayers are requests made to God to do something, or for a specific need or desire to be met. They are intentional requests to God, usually for our personal needs, family needs and ministry or business needs. Their purpose is to appropriate the resources God has made available to us for our daily requirements to be met so we can accomplish His purpose for our lives. The model example of this is in what we call the Lord's prayer in Matt 6:9–13, 'Give us this day our daily bread'.

When we present our petitions to Him we need to have the right motive for asking and not ask 'amiss'. We also need to be single minded and confident in His willingness and ability to supply our provision when we present our requests. We should remember that even though God knows what our needs are before we even ask (Matt 6:8), we are still to ask. Think of James the apostle saying, "you have not because you do not ask" (James 4:23), or Paul commanding us not to worry and to present our prayers and petitions to God (Phil 4:6–7). The basis of petition prayer is that it is prayer that is prayed to a loving Father who cares for us, provides for us, and delights in granting us our prayer requests.

Prayers of Consecration

Consecrate: formal dedication to a sacred purpose. There are times in our lives when we reach a crossroad and wish to make a specific commitment to God. We commit everything to God in these prayers. So this a completely different type of prayer to petition.

Jesus prayed prayers of consecration in the garden of Gethsemane just before He went to the cross. He prayed for the will of God to be done in His life (see Matt 26:36–46). He was consecrating Himself to do the will of God, regardless of His personal feelings or desires.

Prayers of Faith

This prayer is based on knowing what the will of God is through the word, or a specific promise that HE has given, and then praying for and receiving that solution or outcome. The key for this type of prayer is that it's prayed once, with boldness, and in full confidence God will deliver. You don't pray, "If it is your will Father can I have whatever." That is not praying in faith as per James 1:5–6. You pray and believe you have received from God and thank Him for it (Mark 11:24). You might say, for example, "Father I thank you that I can ask for .... in faith and I thank You it is given me." You thank Him and Keep thanking Him that it is granted and that you have it, even if you haven't seen it in the natural realm yet. Keep praising Him and thanking Him for it. The following are scriptures to study in this regard: Mark 11:12–14; Mark 11:20–25; Luke 7:1–10; James 5:13–18; Matt 9:18–26;

Prayers of Intercession

Intercession is "an act of mediation, entreaty, a prayer or petition on behalf of another" (Webster's Dictionary). Our intercessory prayers are the ones that can change the destinies of people, families, businesses and nations. This is the most common type of prayer we see in the Bible. Prayers of intercession were prayed by Abraham, Moses, Daniel, Ezekiel, Isaiah, Amos and many others. If we follow the life of Paul through the New Testament we see most of his prayers are intercessions for others. He prays for the Ephesians in Chap1:17–19 and Chap 3:14–19. In Chapter 6:18 he commands the Ephesians to pray and interceed for all the saints with all manner of prayer.

In Phil 1:9–10 we see more intercession prayer of Paul, and even more in Col 1:3–12. Then it is Epaphras in Col 4:12 doing the praying. There are many more instances of this intercession prayer in the Bible. This is the most important prayer we can be involved in. It is a part of the work of the sons of God. In Heb 7:25 we see that this is what Jesus does. The word tells us that because He intercedes, He is able to save to the uttermost forever those who come to God through Him. This is very important. Did you see that? I repeat, because He intercedes He is able to save to the uttermost for all time those who come to God through Him. This clearly shows the importance of intercession in the successful and eternal salvation of the saints. In the next chapter there will be more on the intercession ministry of the Lord Jesus Christ and the part we play in it.

Travail or Birthing Prayers

The art of labouring or Travailing in the Spirit needs to be restored to the church. This is truly praying with God. Travail can be such an intense praying with God that loud cries, tears, moanings and groanings of great intensity accompany this type of prayer in the Spirit. Heb 5:7. 1 Kings 18:42. An example of this happened a few years ago. I was amongst a group that was gathering to pray. We did this regularly. Suddenly one of the young men who was standing with us fell to the floor clutching his stomach and he started to groan with what seemed to be all his strength. It seemed as if he was dying. Fortunately we knew what was happening and were not alarmed. After a long time he stopped groaning and just lay on the floor peacefully. The prayer burden or labour was prayed through. The thing God wanted brought into the world was birthed.

In the time of Charles Finney this was a common occurrence. Often when sitting down for a meal one of his prayer team would rush from the table to their room as a similar burden would come on them and they would have to pray through to be released of the intense pressure that they were experiencing.

Recently at the end of 2014 a group of intercessors met in Portugal for an extended time of prayer. We got deeper and deeper into prayers and intercessions in the Holy Spirit. After a few days of this, one of the ladies with us started to groan in the pangs of travail. This got more and more intense. Eventually she was crying out loudly in the pangs of labour. Others in the team gathered around her to assist in the prayer pangs. This was prayer of extreme intensity and pressure. Finally with a very loud cry she delivered what the Holy Spirit was birthing. There was a sense of relief and quiet joy in the team when that was concluded.

God is looking for those who would yield their bodies a living sacrifice to Him. That we would go all the way with God in these things. Labour pains, travail and birthing have been discouraged in the church. This is either because of ignorance of Spiritual things or fear of excess.

This is what God has to say about it. In 66:8–9

"Who has heard of such a thing? Who has seen such a thing? Shall a land be borne in one day? Or shall a nation be brought forth in a moment? For as soon as Zion was in labour, she brought forth her children.

Shall I bring to the moment of birth and not cause to bring forth? says the Lord. Shall I Who causes to bring forth shut the womb? Says your God."

Notice how the Lord says it is not He Who blocks the birthing of what is to be brought forth. So what is the problem then? The church generally has lost the ability to recognise the beginning of birth pangs and how to birth the things of God. This is because this is a spiritual activity. Paul says in 1 Cor 14:14,

"If I pray in an unknown tongue, my spirit by the Holy Spirit within me prays, but my mind is unproductive,"

Yielding to the Spirit and praying in tongues is the first step into travail. As you yield to the Spirit He starts to pray with all manner of prayer and entreaty with and through you. Rom 12:1 says that we are to present our bodies a living sacrifice to God which is our reasonable service. As we start to pray in tongues this is exactly what we are doing. Our spirit prays by the Holy Spirit within us. 1Cor 14:14. The more we yield to Him the more He prays through us. The prayer waves of the Spirit quicken in us. And then we start to go into the deeper travails and cries of the Spirit. These are not intellectually initiated and prayed prayers, but come from deep within us.

So as the church yields to the Spirit we will see more and more of this prayer.

This prayer increases the supply of the Holy Spirit to empower and bring about what has been birthed in prayer. An example of this is Elijah on the mountain in 1 Kings 18:42. He birthed what had been prophesied, "Behold I hear the sound of the abundance of rain." When the birthing process was complete, a cloud the size of a man's fist appeared over the sea and soon a hard rain was falling upon them. In the book of James 5:16 we are told that it was because Elijah prayed (or travailed) that this happened.

In Gal 4:19 we see Paul in travail for Christ to be formed in the Galatians. Prophecy and good teaching of the Word must be accompanied with travail. The same can be seen in Col 4:12.

"Epaphras, who is one of your number, a bondslave of Jesus Christ, sends you his greetings, always labouring earnestly for you in his prayers, that you may stand perfect and fully assured in all the will of God. For I bear him witness that he has a deep concern for you and for those who are in Laodicea and Hierapolis."

Prayers for Healing

In the Bible we see Jesus healing the sick. He says in John 14:12 that anyone who believes in Him will do the works He does and greater works.

Jesus healed in many ways. By spitting, by commanding, by laying on of hands and by instructing. So we must be open to the Spirit in this regard. We must ask in prayer how He wants healing ministered. Most times we simply lay hands on the sick as per Mark 16:18 and command sickness and infirmity to leave them. It is not necessary to ask the Father whether it is His will to heal. Scripture is clear Healing is part of the atonement 1 Peter 2:24. We don't need to ask the Father for something He has already given us. It is a done deal.

Here is an example of how we can pray a prayer for Healing. "Father You have given healing in the atonement, so we declare your word to this sickness." "Sickness! by His stripes I/we/he/she is/am healed now bow your knee and leave immediately."

How do we know which prayers to pray and how to pray them? Many times we don't! However the Holy Spirit always does, and that is why our instruction from Paul is to "pray in the Spirit", that is in other tongues. The Spirit will pray all the above mentioned prayers with you. He is your Helper.

When I pray, I pray in the Spirit and then in my understanding, and then in the Spirit and back in my understanding, aware of some of the rules of prayer just mentioned.

In Eph 6, quoted previously, Paul tells us to pray all manner of prayers 'in the Spirit'. From my experience of prayer meetings and individual's prayers, most Christians pray first in their own language and then maybe in the Spirit, if at all. But Paul tells us to do it the other way around.

1 Cor 14:13–15,

"Therefore the person who speaks in an unknown tongue should pray for the power to interpret and explain what he says. For if I pray in an unknown tongue, my spirit by the Holy Spirit within me prays but mind is unproductive. Then what am I to do? I ***will pray with my spirit by the the Holy Spirit*** *that is within me but I* ***will also pray with my mind and understanding****." (Amplified Bible).*

You can go to any football stadium in the world today and observe the crowd at the game. They all know the rules of the game they are watching, and they all understand the flows and moves of the game. Each group of supporters will shout and applaud at the right times and possibly keep quiet at other times. There is an atmosphere of unity and excitement there amongst a team's supporters especially when their team is winning. They energise their team with their support. They are part of the game and keep going back to these games over and over again.

This is how Christian prayer meetings should be. Every person attending should be a part of the team. Each person knowing both the rules of the game they are involved in and how to play it. The idea of every prayer meeting should be to enforce defeat on the opposition. Go to enforce the victory we already have. If we go to our prayer "matches" strong in the Lord and in His mighty power, we will come away from our meetings in full victory every time.

CHAPTER SIX

THE INTERCESSION MINISTRY OF JESUS

In the book of Rom 8:34 we are told that Jesus, Who is at the right hand of God, intercedes for the saints. This is also mentioned in the book of Hebrews.

Heb 7:25 *"Therefore He is able to save to the uttermost those who come to God through Him, since He always lives to make intercession for them."*

The above scripture in Hebrews, makes an astounding statement. It states the reason He is able to save to the "uttermost" is because He intercedes for the saints. "Uttermost" means completely, perfectly, finally and for all time. Intercession, which we defined in the previous chapter, is to pray or petition on behalf of another. So because of the the intercession prayer of Jesus, He is able to save us all, for all time. Obviously this intercession prayer of Jesus is a vital part in the complete eternal salvation of the body of Christ.

We are going to examine what this means to us in more detail in this chapter.

To begin with in this section we will look at the relationship between the Father, Jesus and the Holy Spirit, and ourselves, who are in Christ. By understanding that we are part of this relationship we can then look at and understand how Jesus working with the Holy Spirit and us, intercedes for the saints.

We are in Christ, One with Him.

Jesus says these things about His relationship with the Father in the passages below: John10:30, *"I and the Father are one."*

John 14:9–10, *"The Father who lives in Me does the works."*

John14:3, *"I will take you to Myself that where I am you may be also."*

Now where is Jesus? He is in the Father verse 10. If we are where He is, John 14:3, then we are also in the Father.

John 14:20, *"When that day comes you will know for yourselves that I am in My Father and you are in Me and I am in you."*

We are in Jesus, He's in the Father, therefore, because we are in Him we are also in the Father and He's in us.

Look at what Paul writes in Col 2:10, *"And **you are in Him** made full and having come to fullness of life in Christ you too are filled with the Godhead – Father Son and Holy Spirit – and reach full spiritual stature." (Amplified Bible).*

We are in Jesus, Who is in the Father, and the Father, Jesus and the Holy Spirit are in us. Whether we feel it or not, that scripture is saying the fullness of the Godhead is in us. This is truth that I choose right now to believe. You choose to believe it now as well. **God is in me! God is in you!** Now we know why Jesus said in Matt 11:11,

"Assuredly I say to you that among men born of women there has not risen one greater than John the Baptist but he who is least in the kingdom is greater than John the Baptist."

When we understand and accept that God is in us, we don't need to continually ask for more power or ask God to "send His power". Rather, we need to release the mighty power of God that is already within us. This is what sons of God do. This is how the sons of God will be revealed! Choose to believe that Col 2:10 applies to you.

The New Testament overflows with scripture that reinforces the truth of our being in and one with Christ. Here are more scriptures that show we are in Him and the Godhead is in us. John 17:21, *"That they also may be one in Us"*

1 Cor 6:17, *"Those who join themselves to the Lord become one spirit with Him."*

Eph 5:31–32 speaks of a man and a woman becoming one, but Paul says this is a picture of Christ and the church.

John 15:4–6 He's the vine, we are the branches.

If we are in Jesus and He's in us, then we do what He does! Apart from Him we can do nothing. We are joined to Him. We are His body.

Paul tells us in Gal 2:20 *"I have been crucified with Christ; it is no longer I who live, but Christ lives in me; and the life I now live in the flesh I live by faith in the Son of God who loved me and gave Himself up for me."*

If we are one with Him, seated in Him in heavenly places, have His mind, and if we are His body, and it is not us who live but Christ in us who lives, then we are completely a part of Him. So whatever He does we do. If He ever lives to intercede for the saints we do the same! He does His intercession with, in, and through us.

Apart from Him we can do nothing! But in Him, joined to Him, we do what He does. Likewise if we do things in His name, He does what we do. We are going to look at how Jesus prayed in the Old Covenant to further grasp and understand how we, the saints today, are to pray His prayers of intercession.

The Old Testament Intercession Ministry of Jesus

We need to understand the dynamics and expression of the prayers that Jesus prayed in the Old Covenant. Remember even though Jesus has been born again (Rom 8:29), He hasn't changed in what He does . The Covenants haven't changed God, they have changed the way He relates to us. He still expresses prayer the same way, but now He does it through and with us by His Spirit. He's the same yesterday, today and forever, Heb 13:8. We are the ones who have changed. In the New Covenant we have been crucified and raised to new life in Him. We are now seated in Him in heavenly places thanks to the cross and His shed blood. We relate differently to God compared to the way Old Covenant people did. We need to see ourselves in Him. As you read the following scriptures see yourself joined to Him and doing what He is doing in those scriptures with Him.

Jesus as intercessor, Isaiah 59:16–17,

"And He saw that there was no man and wondered that there was no intercessor (no-one to intervene on behalf of truth and right) therefore His own arm brought Him victory and His own righteousness (having the Spirit without measure) sustained Him. For the Lord put on righteousness as a breastplate or coat of mail, and salvation as a helmet upon His head; He put on garments of vengeance for clothing and was clad with zeal and furious divine jealousy as a cloak." (Amplified Bible).

The armour that Jesus put on is, the same armour that we are told to told to put on in Eph 6:13–16 by Paul to engage in spiritual warfare. It is the armour of God.

Jesus in warfare, Isaiah 42:13–14:

"The Lord will go forth like a mighty man, He will rouse up His zealous indignation and vengeance like a warrior: He will cry, yes, He will shout aloud, He will do mightily against His enemies."

Look at: "He will shout aloud", the word shout is ruwa. It is used to describe the shrill, clear cry or roar of a battle cry. It is like the powerful roar of a lion.

Did you know the Lord shouts a battle cry and He roars like a lion.

The roar of a lion intimidates his enemies and paralyses his prey. It calls his own to him and proclaims, "This is my territory!" In Christ we have the roar of the Lion of Judah? He still shouts and roars today through us. The shout of the Lord is a very powerful spiritual weapon.

In Num 23:21 Balem cannot curse Israel because they have the "Shout of the Lord" in their midst. *"The shout of praise to their King is among the people" (Amplified Bible).*

The word shout here is also *"ruwa"*. It also means, *"To split the ears with sound, an ear splitting shout, war cry, shout in triumph, shout in applause, to raise a noise by shouting or with an instrument."*

When the shout of the Lord is released through us, it is like throwing an atomic bomb into the spirit realm. Demons are scattered and smashed about, strongholds are smashed and the heavens are opened. It was the shout "ruwa" of the Lord that brought the walls of Jericho down. (Joshua 6:16 and verse 20). It still brings walls down today. It still destroys strongholds of the enemy today.

Recently I attended a Christian International meeting with Dr Bill Hamon and Dr Sharon Stone in the UK. Dr Hamon instructed the congregation to shout the "shout" of the Lord which we did for about five minutes. The result was phenomenal, we forced open the heaven and released the new move of God in Britain. The change in the atmosphere in that place was tangible. This new move Dr Hamon has called the Day of the Saints. This world wide move of God has begun. It is the saints equipped, mobilised and doing the work of the ministry.

Jesus in Travail Isaiah 42:14.

"Thus says the Lord I have for a long time held My peace, I have been still and restrained Myself. Now I will cry out like a woman in travail, I will gasp and pant together." (Amplified Bible).

Here we read that Jesus is birthing or travailing in the Spirit. We see both Elijah in 1 Kings 18:44 and Paul in Gal 4:19 doing this. Paul speaks of how he is again in travail or pangs of birth that Christ be formed in the Galatians. A lot more travailing prayer is needed in the church today.

Travail is essential for people to be born again and for Christ to be formed in them once they are born again. When we examine the prayers of Paul that are recorded in his writings we see that most of them were for the saints he was writing to and not for himself.

Jesus in the days of His flesh Heb 5:7,

"In the days of His flesh Jesus offered up prayers and supplications with loud/strong cries and tears to Him who was able to save Him out from death, and He was heard because of His Godly fear."

"Strong" means: mightily, forcibly, violently. "Crying" means: cry out, cry for vengeance.

Let us stir ourselves in the Holy Spirit and do the same. Let us shout the shout of the Lord! Let us gasp and pant with the Holy Spirit!

The Intercession ministry of Jesus today

In Heb 7:25 and Rom 8:34 we see that the Glorified Lord Jesus is interceding for the saints. A vital part of this ministry of the Lord Jesus is the human experience that He brings into it. The Holy Spirit has never been human nor has the Father. Jesus has first hand experience of what it is to face the devil and temptation as a human. He was able to do this without sin, even though He felt the pull and response of His flesh to temptation. He understands what we face in the flesh and yet He is fully God. This makes Him able to intercede for us as both man and God and bring to the Godhead this understanding of what we as humans both face and need. Heb 4:15,

"For we do not have a High Priest Who is unable to understand and sympathize and have a shared feeling with our weaknesses and infirmities and liability to the assaults of temptation, but One Who has been tempted in every respect as we are, yet without sinning." Amplified Bible.

Let us look briefly at our relationship with the Godhead again, and then we can consider the process of how we are engaged in the intercession ministry of Jesus.

We are in Him

We are in Him and He is in us. The Holy Spirit is in us. The Father is in us Col 2:10. Our relationship with God is so close that we the church are called the body of Christ (Eph 1:22–23). Now my own body does what I do. In the same way the body of Christ does what He does. The One Who connects us to our Heavenly Father and Jesus is the Holy Spirit. The Holy Spirit is also involved in the intercession ministry of Jesus. The Holy Spirit intercedes for the saints (Rom 8:26 – 27) through us. The Spirit is in us! Jesus is in us! We cannot separate ourselves from the intercession prayer ministry for the saints of Jesus and the Holy Spirit, because we are in them and they are in us. The Holy Spirit takes from what is Jesus' and reveals it to us. He draws the perspective of the human experience from Jesus as He prays the intercession prayers of Jesus through us to the Father.

And then Rom 8:28 applies, *"We are assured and know that God being a partner in their labour all things work together and are fitting into a plan for good to and for those who love Him and are called according to His design and purpose." Amplified Bible.*

The role of the Church in the Intercession ministry of Jesus

In 2 Cor 5:14–15 Paul tells us we are not to live for ourselves but we are to live for Christ. In fact in Gal 2:20 He goes so far as to say, "It is not I who live, but Christ in me who lives."

If Christ ever lives to intercede for the saints, that is what we the Church should be doing!

Paul commands this in Eph 6:18, *"Pray at all times on every occasion in every season in the Spirit with all manner of prayer and entreaty. To that end keep alert and watch with strong perseverance interceding on behalf of all the saints God's consecrated people."* (Amplified Bible).

This praying in the Spirit for all the saints is further explained in Rom 8:26.

"We don't know what to pray or how to offer our prayer worthily but the Spirit makes intercessions for us with groanings which cannot be uttered." He does this through us. We join with Him and we release the utterance and groanings He gives us out our mouths.

The next verse says, *"the Spirit intercedes for the saints in perfect harmony with God's will."* The Spirit can do this because He knows the thoughts and plans of God for every saint.
1 Cor 2:10. "the Spirit searches the deep things of God."

So praying together with and in the Holy Spirit we are now a part of the intercession ministry of the Lord Jesus Christ. In praying in the Spirit we also tap into the power of God in our prayer.

Praying in the Holy Spirit we have victory.

This next scripture shows what happens as we join with the Holy Spirit, against the enemy. Isaiah 59:19,

"When the enemy shall come in like a flood, the Spirit of the Lord will lift up a standard against him and put him to flight, for He (the Spirit)

will come like a rushing stream which the breath of the Lord drives." (Amplified Bible).

The rushing stream is like a great spiritual river in flood. As we all allow the rivers of the Spirit that flow from within us to be combined into one by the Holy Spirit, we will push away anything that comes against us or our brethren, or attempts to hinder the advance of the Kingdom of God. We can do this because He, the Holy Spirit, takes a hold of together with us against whatever we are dealing with.

Here is the Strong's Concordance definition of the "Breath" of the Lord.

The "Breath" that drives the rushing stream is "ruach". It means; "wind, breath, Spirit, Spirit of God, Imparting a warlike energy and executive and administrative power."

This is exactly what happens in and through us as the Holy Spirit energizes us. We get this warlike energy and release the administrative power and decree the word of God with executive authority.

Warfare Praise

Another weapon of the Spirit against the enemy is warfare praise. Here are two references to this. Isaiah 30:32,

"And every passing stroke of the staff of punishment and doom which the Lord lays upon them shall be to the sound of Israel's timbrels and lyres, when in battle He attacks with swinging and menacing arms." (Amplified Bible).

Psa 149:6–9.

"Let the high praises of God be in their throats and a two edged sword in their hands

To wreak vengeance upon the nations and chastisement upon the peoples

to bind their kings with fetters of iron. To execute upon them the judgement written."

In conclusion, earlier in the book we saw that when Jesus asked Saul why he was persecuting Him, He showed how unified His church is with Him. What the disciples were doing He was doing. What happened to them, happened to Him. Likewise What He is doing now we are doing.

We engage in His prayer life? With violence, zeal and intense exertion Matt 11:11–12.

By allowing the Holy Spirit to control us and lead us into this.

The Holy Spirit will pray through us that which He hears from the Father, and this is why He will pray the perfect will of God for the saints with and through us.

1 Cor 2:11, *"no one discerns (comes to know and comprehend) the thoughts of God except the Spirit of God."*

Rom 8:27, *"The Spirit intercedes and pleads before God in behalf of the saints according to and in harmony with God's will."*

CHAPTER SEVEN

ACTIVATING THE SPIRIT OF PRAYER THROUGH TONGUES

A key feature of praying with God is that prayer becomes one of the most exciting things we do. It is full of life, dynamic, explosive, meaningful, fulfilling and produces transformation. It is a spiritual activity.

So how do we take our prayer lives and prayer meetings from dull hard work to these powerful and exciting times?

The answer is that it is a journey that begins with understanding and praying in the gift of tongues.

In this chapter we will discuss how to activate ourselves in the gift of tongues so that we can join in with the prayer ministry of the Holy Spirit. Do not be put off by false teaching that "tongues and miracles have passed away" and that these were just for the times of the apostles of Jesus Christ and the early church, or, that tongues are for today but not for everyone. I have even heard an internationally known bible teacher teach that "Tongues are of the devil".

We will let the Word of God be our source of information and final authority in regards to praying in tongues.

Mark 16:17–18 clearly states,

"these signs will follow those who believe,

They will drive out demons, ***they will speak in new tongues****."*

If we believe in Jesus Christ and the Word of God the above verse means we will also do these things. It does not say, "some who believe" or "the first few who believe." It applies to all who believe. Speaking in other tongues is clearly a biblical activity that every believer should accept and participate in.

Tongues stirs up your spirit in the Holy Spirit

In 1 Cor 14:4 Paul the apostle writes,

"He who speaks in a strange tongue edifies and improves himself,"

What this means is that you build up or charge your own spirit. An example of this is that as a motor car is being driven, the alternator attached to its engine charges or edifies and improves its battery.

In the book of Jude verse 20 we see the same thing mentioned.

"But you beloved, build yourselves up founded on your most holy faith make progress rise like an edifice higher and higher, praying in the Holy Spirit."

It is important we do this because we need to be charged and full of energy and power to face the demands of life.

Paul tells us clearly that in 1 Cor 14:2 that the one who speaks in tongues utters secret truths and hidden things in the Holy Spirit. Another way of putting this is, "He who speaks in tongues is praying in the Holy Spirit."

Paul is so convinced of the benefit of "charging" himself in the Holy Spirit that in 1 Cor 14:18 he writes,

"I thank God I speak in tongues more than any of you or all of you put together."

Why does Paul do this? He does this because he knows the benefits of doing this. Praying in tongues stirs your spirit up in the Holy Spirit! It **activates** your spirit. It builds you up in your inner man and renews you in the spirit of your mind.

In fact if you persist in praying in tongues, you will be so stirred up and charged in the Holy Spirit that the Holy Spirit will start to overflow out of you.

Jesus said in John 7:38 that rivers of living water would flow from the innermost beings of those that believed in Him.

Many people in the world do not know about the spiritual blessings and principles of God. They are not pursuing God. However, in doctor's rooms across the world there are people seeking healing from their distresses and sicknesses. In addiction clinics and all types of places of counselling, desperate people are looking for relief and answers. There are answers for all these needs.

The answers are in the Word of God and the rivers of God which flow from the innermost beings of those who believe. That is why each believer needs to activate these rivers that are within them by speaking in tongues.

The gift of tongues was the very first gift given to the early church. This gift is the key to all the other gifts given to us by the Lord Jesus Christ. As we flow in the gift of tongues the other gifts are also stirred.

We need to activate all the blessings and rivers of God in our lives, to meet our own needs as well as the needs of others. This will glorify Jesus in the world and show His goodness and kindness to all. It is the goodness and kindness of God that brings people to repentance and salvation.

In the next section we are going to look at activating and flowing in the the gift of tongues

Activating the gift of tongues

The gifts and manifestations of God are activated. As we understand how we got saved we can use the same understanding to unlock the gift of tongues.

We had to activate our salvation when we heard the gospel. It was not enough to hear the word and believe. We had to act on what we had heard when we heard the gospel. How? We believed first and then confessed with our mouths our faith in the Lord Jesus Christ. Rom 10:9–10.

So we activated our salvation by speaking out our mouths our faith in the Lord Jesus Christ.

We received the gift (baptism) of the Holy Spirit through the laying on of hands. See Acts 19:6, Acts 10:44, Acts 8:17. Also Acts 9:17.

We then had to activate what we received by speaking out our mouths as the Spirit gave us utterance.

In Acts 2:1–4 we see that when the Spirit came, all present in the room were filled and began to speak in other tongues. Not one in that room was left out. Just so today, not one of us should be left out of this experience. This was the very first activation in the lives of the disciples after their salvation. When the Spirit came and they were filled, they started speaking in tongues with the ability to speak in languages they did not know. They did the speaking as the Spirit gave them the utterance.

Activate this gift in your life now

If you have not experienced the baptism of the Holy Spirit with speaking in tongues do not wait another day. Some of you just need to start speaking in tongues as the Spirit has already come on you. **You need to speak, you need to activate this gift in you.** He will give you the utterance. Even if you have only one word, use that over and over until another one comes. Don't let your mind tell you things like "This is silly. This is gibberish; you are just making this up". This is your spirit praying by the Holy Spirit, it is not initiated in your mind but it is from the Holy Spirit giving your spirit utterance.

Jesus said in John 7:38 that rivers of living water would flow from the innermost beings of those who believed in Him. How do rivers start? They start as springs! Take the little you have got and work with it. Work with it. Exercise it. Practice with it. Allow it to flow. It will open up and open up and open up. Do not be like the boy in the children's story, who put his finger in the small hole in the dyke and thus prevented the hole being enlarged by the water flowing through it. The whole town would have been flooded if he had not done this. We want to do the opposite. We want to allow the small trickle to enlarge

Water builds up power as trickles flow together to become streams, streams flow together to become rivers, rivers flow together to become unstoppable torrents. The floods in Cornwall shown on National TV in the UK a few years ago showed this very clearly. Cars were swept away, roads were swept away and even bridges were swept away.

Praying in tongues is not natural

We must not allow our minds and reason, which are the "little boy's finger", to block up the trickle starting from our innermost beings as we pray in tongues before it can become a mighty river flowing from within us.

Our minds, if un-renewed, want to keep us working in the natural and seen realm using natural wisdom. 1 Cor 2:12–14. This is why we are told not to look to the seen but to the unseen realm in 2 Cor 4:18.

Our natural minds say, "Seeing is believing," our spirits say, "Believing is seeing." Our natural minds tell us that praying in tongues is silly, useless, embarrassing, and not necessary. However, our spirits are energized and strengthened by praying in tongues.

Activating Tongues

We are to activate these rivers in our lives. In 2 Tim 1:6–7 Paul reminds Timothy to stir (activate) up the fire of God that is in him, which is the Spirit of Power, Love and a Sound Mind. Look at what God has given Timothy, and note that the same blessings apply to each one of us because we have all been given every spiritual blessing there is in Christ Jesus. Eph 1:3.

However, these gifts and blessings have to be stirred up! They are stirred up by a combination of declaration and praying in tongues. Paul does this in his own life by speaking in tongues 'more than all of the Corinthians put together'.1 Cor:14:18. He prays in tongues and then declares the Word.

At Pentecost, the first activation in the Church was the river of tongues. This was a supernatural activation not a natural activation.

This is a simple gift to activate. As we begin and continue to pray in tongues the Spirit will get involved with us. We can turn this activity on or off at will. **It is an act of our will to pray in tongues or not to pray in tongues.**

Benefits of Praying in tongues

We must persevere with praying in tongues to stir up and release rivers of living water from our innermost beings. Do not stop until you start to enjoy the benefits of your effort.

We have spiritual senses just as we have natural senses, and one of the benefits of praying in tongues will be to sharpen and develop our spiritual senses. These spiritual senses are taste, touch, smell, hearing and sight. Heb 5:14,

"But solid food is for full grown men, for those whose senses and mental faculties are trained by practice to discriminate and distinguish between

what is morally good and noble and what is evil and contrary to either divine or human law."

The spiritual senses are not to be confused with our natural senses. They may seem the same but they are not. In John 5:19 Jesus says He can only do what He sees His Father doing. This is spiritual sight. In John 5:30 Jesus hears God to make His decisions. In John 10:16 Jesus says His sheep will listen to His voice. In Mark 5:28–30 we see a woman touch Jesus in faith. This was a spiritual touch different to all the others in the crowd who were physically touching Jesus. The other two spiritual senses we have are taste and smell. We are told to taste the Lord and see He is good Psa 34:8, and Paul speaks about the fragrance of Christ 2 Cor 2:14–15.

Another benefit of praying in tongues is that our spirits will be energized and our faith built up. Jude 20 says,

"But you beloved build yourselves up founded on your most holy faith make progress rise like an edifice higher and higher, praying in the Holy Spirit." (Amplified Bible).

Spiritual things will then start to make more sense to us and we will not allow the "finger" of natural reason to stop the activation of true wisdom and revelation in our lives. We will start to interpret spiritual language with spiritual understanding 1 Cor 2:13. The rivers will flow!

Why we need to be activated in tongues

- To charge and empower our spirits. 1 Cor 14:4, 2 Tim 1:6–7. Isaiah 40:31
- Most Christians run from conference to conference to receive impartation and be built up by others because they have not learned to build themselves up in the Holy Spirit. Their strength comes from outside them and not from the mighty power that is at work in and for

them. Eph 1:17–19. We need both stirring and impartation to build ourselves up. To bless with our spirits. 1 Cor 14:16

- To be built up in our faith Jude :20
- To increase the influence of the Holy Spirit upon us. To get used to Him, the way He speaks, the way He feels, the way He prays through us.1 Cor 14:14–15. The way He leads us Rom 8:14. Humility is saying Lord I trust You, lead me, show me what is to come.
- To step into the supernatural through revelation 1 Cor 2:13. 1 Cor 14:13. To pray the perfect will of God with God, the Holy Spirit. Rom 8:26–27.
- To move into the realm of true warfare in the Spirit. Isaiah 59:16. Num 23:21.
- To be strengthened in our inner man to grasp and experience the love of God Eph 3:16. To go beyond our natural limitations. Eph 3:20. The power at work within us is the Holy Spirit energizing us as we pray in the Holy Spirit.
- To be strong in the Lord and His mighty power. Eph 6:10.

Different Kinds of tongues

Scripture shows us a whole range of different kinds of tongues.

1. Personal prayer language to speak mysteries to God and build ourselves up. 1 Cor 14:2 and Jude:20.
2. Unknown languages of men. Acts 2 and 1 Cor 13:1.
3. Tongues of angels 1 Cor 13:1.
4. Tongues and interpretation in gifts of the Holy Spirit 1 Cor 12:10.
5. Prayer language of the Holy Spirit Himself. Rom 8:27
6. Language of blessing. 1 Cor 14:16.

7. Language of thanksgiving. 1 Cor 14:16
8. Language of the Spirit, expressing spiritual truths, which are to be interpreted for revelation. 1 Cor 2:13.

We can activate and experience all of these. By praying in tongues we stir and edify and activate ourselves in the Holy Spirit.

Praying in tongues greatly increases the influence of the Holy Spirit upon us.

In concluding this section it is essential that we pray in tongues as it greatly increases the influence of the Holy Spirit upon us and increases our understanding of how God thinks and works.

1 Cor 14:14–15

" *For if I pray in an unknown tongue, my spirit by the Holy Spirit within me prays, but my mind is unproductive, it bears no fruit and helps nobody.*

Then what am I to do? I will pray with my spirit by the Holy Spirit that is within , but I will also pray with my mind and understanding."

When I pray, I pray first in the Spirit in tongues and then in my understanding because this is the order we are told to pray in by Paul in the above scripture. If only the Church would do their prayer meetings this way. While I am praying in tongues I am also praying with my mind. We can do this because the two types of prayer come from different parts of our being. For example you can write a letter while praying in tongues, but if you are praying in your understanding while trying to write a letter, it is very difficult if not impossible. One or the other activity stops while the other is being done.

So praying with my mind takes place in my thoughts while my mouth is speaking out the utterances of the Holy Spirit. I lock my mind onto the tongues I am speaking. Are they loud or soft? Are they violent? Am I birthing or travailing? Am I blessing or giving thanks? Am I worshipping? Am I decreeing the word of God? Am I releasing things?

Whatever is happening as I pray in the Holy Spirit, I am alert and watchful in my mind and asking continually, "Lord Spirit, what are we doing." I am literally doing what it says to do in 1 Cor 14:13 asking for the understanding of what is being prayed. The Holy Spirit loves to show us what He is doing.

This has resulted in me having all kinds of adventures and experiences with God. Perhaps the greatest benefit of this is I grow in understanding and experience of the love and awesomeness of God.

What I am speaking about is for all of us. The more you work with the gift of tongues the more you will see and experience the importance of this ability God has given us.

CHAPTER EIGHT

PRACTICALITIES OF PRAYING IN THE HOLY SPIRIT

I want to establish some practical principles for successful intercession. Perhaps two of the greatest issues we have to address as intercessors are:

1. True unity of spirit and purpose,
2. What the spirit of religion has done to our thinking.

The issue of unity

If we were to get twenty mature Christians together to decree governmentally into their county school program, some of the possible issues that would arise could be:

Should the schools be privatised?

Should faith schools be allowed?

What about parents who want to home school?

Should we have a grammar school?

Should pupils be bussed in from less privileged areas?

What about the carbon footprint?

There is potential here for conflicting prayers and decrees to be made. Why is this?

Generally Christians pray from their own perspective, intellect and understanding.

What would happen if using this same scenario we set some ground rules:

1. God is bigger smarter and wiser than us. Let us find His mind on these matters and say only what He shows us.
2. We want our prayers to be not only accurate, but also presented correctly, so we will allow the Holy Spirit to pray in and through us.

The above two conditions if agreed upon, would create the necessary agreement and will to work in unity in this matter even if some of the people praying had strongly held and opposing views. This would negate the need for "Democracy" and everyone to express their strongly held point of view, which ultimately causes division and fragmentation in the Body of Christ.

So if we can go beyond our personal prayer language into the prayer language of the Holy Spirit (Intercessor), we partner with the Holy Spirit (God), to pray the perfect will of God for that situation. We allow the Holy Spirit to orchestrate and conduct the prayer until the job is done. We know when He is satisfied the job is done because He gives us the title deed to the prayer – that is the peace of God. Phil 4:7.

We know that Jesus ever lives to intercede for the saints Heb 7:25, and He came as an intercessor Isaiah 59:16–17.

He wants us His body involved in His ministry of intercession. But He wants us to do this in Unity with Him and with one another.

So how does He do this?

He said He would send another Comforter, Helper, Advocate , Standby, Strengthener, Counsellor, INTERCESSOR to be with us John 16:7 (Amplified).

The Holy Spirit is the One who directs the prayers God wants prayed on this earth through His people. The Spirit prays with and through those who will yield to Him.

If we read Rom 8:26, the Word says that the Spirit helps us in our weakness (or inability) for we do not know what prayer to pray nor how to pray it worthily.

That word "helps" is the Greek word "sunantilambanomai" which means, "He takes hold of together with us against!"

If the Holy Spirit is allowed to work through us like this then Rom 8:28 applies.

"We are assured and know that God being a partner in their labour, all things work together for the good of those who love God and are called according to His design and purpose".

Read Col 4:12. Paul calls this type of prayer labour. So the labour referred to here, is the labour of praying in partnership with the Holy Spirit. And by involving God in the issues prayed for, there will be a favourable outcome.

Rom 8:27 says, "The Spirit intercedes and pleads before God on behalf of the Saints in perfect accordance with God's will." How does He do this?

The best way He does this, is by inspiring us in our prayer language, and giving us utterance.

1 Cor 14:14 Says,

"If I pray in an unknown tongue, my spirit by the Holy Spirit within prays." (Amplified).

This means we bypass our intellect and understanding. This is an act of the highest humility and trust in God. This is presenting your body a living sacrifice (Rom 12:1). Many people think the Holy Spirit is incapable of doing the job if they do not understand everything that is being prayed.

This causes them not to use their prayer language very much, if at all. In 1 Cor14:18 Paul says he prays in the Spirit more than all the Corinthians put together. (Amplified Bible)

Once we have prayed in the Holy Spirit and discerned the mind of Christ we can pray in the understanding. **Paul says to pray first in the Spirit then in the understanding**. How often do we do it that way around?

At Babel God confused the language of the people. This was to scatter them Gen 11:7–8. In Gen 11:6 God says,

"They are one people with one language, this is only the beginning of what they will do and now nothing they have imagined will be impossible for them."

Once the new Covenant was established, God reverses this by giving people languages inspired by the Holy Spirit Acts 2:4. His plan is to unify all things in Christ Eph1:10. We need to note this and yield to this desire of God. **The language of the Holy Spirit unifies!**

Imagine what is possible to us who believe, when we are in unity with God, and with one another!

As an intercession leader it has been my experience that people can accept what was just discussed but battle with the practical aspect of it.

So we are to partner with God in our prayers!

In childlike trust in Him and not having to work out everything with our limited minds we can do this.

The issue of religion

We cannot partner with God in prayer fully if we are always sin conscious. Adam and Eve hid from God when they became sin conscious. For hundreds of years Christians have been taught by the spirit of religion, that they are sinners, saved by grace and that the heart of man is desperately wicked. For those outside of Christ this is true, but for Christians it is not.

Rom 6:3 says if we have been baptised into Christ Jesus we were baptised into His death. See Rom 6:6. That old sinner, rebel, wicked hearted man died in Christ Jesus. See Gal 2:19 and 20. Now read 2 Cor 5:17 which says if any man be in Christ he is a new creature altogether.

Eph 2:5 tells us that,

"even when we were dead slain in our transgression, He gave us the very same new life with which He raised Christ from the dead and He gave us joint seating with Him in the heavenly sphere."

So as a Christian believer you are a new creature alive with the same Life as Jesus has.

You are not a reconditioned sinner!

You are the righteousness of God in Christ Jesus!

The Father looks at us and Says "Look at My son, look at My daughter aren't they great!" He does this because He reckons the person who did the bad stuff dead, slain in Christ, on the cross (2 Cor 5:14).

God wants us to be bold in His presence and to be worthy ambassadors of Christ. He wants to expand His Kingdom and make His manifold wisdom known to the powers and principalities through us His church (Eph 3:10). We have to carry ourselves as Sons of God and exercise authority as sons of God and His representatives on this earth.

Let us rise up as Ambassadors of Christ in the boldness and power of God!

Imagine one of the Ambassadors of Britain crawling through the door of 10 Downing Street, grabbing the Prime Minister's feet, and with his head on the ground, saying, "O Prime Minister, I am unworthy to stand in your presence!" The Prime Minister would replace him immediately, and so he should.

Do not be an ambassador for Christ who behaves like that! That's pathetic.

We are partners and co-labourers with God. We come to Him boldly. Our prayers are to be God breathed and Spirit prayed. It is His Kingdom, and His perfect will needs to be prayed every time we pray. We can achieve this by praying first in the Spirit and then in the understanding, the order that Paul puts it in 1 Cor 14:13–15.

We have to lay aside our personal agendas and everything we have learned up to now and trust Him to lead us as we pray and intercede in this, the new season we have already entered into.

Rivers of Prayer Power Flowing from Within You

Jesus said in John 7:38,

"He that believes in Me as the scripture has said, from his innermost being shall flow springs and rivers of living water."

We spoke about the rivers that flow out of our innermost being in an earlier chapter. In this section I want to speak specifically about rivers of prayer.

Notice Jesus said in the above quote that it is rivers, plural, and not a river that will flow from our innermost being. The next verse tells us that

He was speaking here of the Holy Spirit who had not yet been given. The qualification for this was to "**believe.**" John 7:38.

Paul picks up on the same theme in Eph 1:19–20 where he is praying for the Ephesians:

"that you may know and understand the immeasurable and surpassing greatness of His power in and for those who believe."

Do you believe that this resurrection power of God is in you?

The place where this power resides is in our innermost beings. **It is there whether you feel it or not.** This is the same power God demonstrated when He raised Jesus from the dead. This power must be released from our innermost being! Each one of us has the capacity to do this.

Releasing these rivers from our innermost beings is not a mental or logical exercise but an exercise of faith and trust in the Holy Spirit. We have spent so much time exercising our minds and intellects in flowing in the things of God, that we have hindered the release of these rivers of God's power from flowing from within us.

Scripture tells us that,

"The weapons of our warfare are not natural weapons but they are mighty through God to the pulling down and overthrow of strongholds." 2 Cor 10:3–6.

Let us get out of our natural ability and into the spiritual arena where the battle really is.

We want to release rivers of prayer power from our innermost beings to change circumstances, release the atmosphere of heaven, birth the promises of God and affect the hearts of those we pray for.

When we pray like this, from our innermost beings, our prayer has the same weight and value with God as the prayers of Jesus, because our Heavenly Father loves us as much as He loves Jesus. (John 17:23). Another reason for this is because this kind of prayer is Holy Spirit inspired, perfectly chosen and perfectly presented to our Father.

This is why Jesus can say the following in John 15:7,

"If you live in Me and My words remain in you and continue to live in your hearts, ask whatever you will and it shall be done for you."

The Holy Spirit helps us to pray

Rom 8:26 tells us,

"We do not know what prayer to offer or how to offer it worthily (correctly)."

Even Paul with all his great revelation writes that he doesn't know what to pray or how to pray what he does pray correctly.

Likewise we do not know what to pray and even if we did, how would we know how to present this right prayer correctly?

But who does know how to do this? The Holy Spirit does. He knows the deep things of God and reveals them to us.

For this reason Jesus sent His Spirit to help us in every prayer we pray. Jesus said in John 16:7,

"I will send another Comforter, Helper, Advocate, Standby, Strengthener, Counsellor, INTERCESSOR to you (to be in close fellowship with you)."

The Spirit knows the deep dreams and plans that God has for our lives. Eph 2:10 says,

"For we are God's own handiwork (His workmanship) recreated in Christ Jesus (born anew) that we may do those good works which God predestined (planned beforehand) for us (taking paths which He prepared ahead of time) that we should walk in them (living the good life which He prearranged and made ready for us to live."

So God has plans and projects for each one of us. We need to know what these are. We need to take the time to find out and then spend some time praying into them and working toward accomplishing them. 1 Cor 2:9,

"Eye has not seen, ear has not heard and has not entered into the heart of man all that God has made and keeps ready for those who love Him."

This continues in verse 10:

"Yet to us God has revealed them by and through His Spirit."

The Holy Spirit is the one who reveals all the plans and purposes and counsel of God to us! Our understanding is limited but the Holy Spirit's understanding is not. That is why we have to pray with and through the Holy Spirit with all manner of prayer in every situation. Eph 6:18.

As we start to pray in the Spirit, He prays the prayers necessary to order events in our lives. How do we get to walk in the paths and do the things God has arranged for us? By praying in and with the Holy Spirit.

Good prayers to pray:

"Father I know that you have prepared paths for me to walk in. I am your workmanship prepared for good works, I know Lord Jesus You are the author and perfecter of my faith and that in and through You I have been given every spiritual blessing in the heavenly realm Eph 1:3. I receive these blessings from your Spirit. I thank you Father I can pray in your Spirit for these blessings to be released into this realm and for circumstances to be ordered for me to be in the right place at the right time and for words to be given me so that I can say the right things when I am in that right place at the right time."

"Holy Spirit would you pray with me and give me utterance in my heavenly language to order my steps and give me wisdom and revelation concerning all that God has prepared for me."

The Holy Spirit directs the prayers we pray to God. He prays perfect prayers with and through those who will yield to Him. It's a partnership! Yes! The Holy Spirit will actually work with us in our prayer lives.

Have you ever asked?

"Holy Spirit, will you please come pray with me and help me to present my petitions and requests to God perfectly?"

We are told to present our petitions and requests to God in Phil 4:6. In Rom 8:26 the Word says that,

"the Spirit helps us in our weakness (or inability), for we do not know what prayer to pray nor how to pray it worthily."

That word "helps" is the Greek word "sunantilambanomai" which means He takes hold of together with us against. What a wonderful thought, I allow Him to use my spirit, soul and body to pray with and through me and I get to ride in the Holy Spirit bulldozer as He comes and pushes mountains out the way. This is like the mouse and elephant that walked across a wooden bridge together. At the other side, the mouse looked up at his friend the elephant and said, "My, we really shook that bridge up didn't we!"

If the Holy Spirit is allowed to work through us like this then Rom 8:28 applies;

"We are assured and know that God being a partner in their labour, all things work together for the good of those who love God and are called according to His design and purpose."

So the labour referred to here, is the labour of praying in **partnership** with the Holy Spirit. And by involving God in the issues prayed for, there will be a favourable outcome.

Can you see why I emphasize that we must partner with God in prayer?

That is exactly what Paul says is the key to successful prayer in Rom 8:28. Prayer that makes all things work to the good of those who love Him.

In Col 4:12 Paul calls this type of prayer labour.

Rom 8:27 says,

"The Spirit intercedes and pleads before God on behalf of the Saints in perfect accordance with God's will."

How does He do this? The best way He does this is by inspiring us in our prayer language (tongues), and giving us utterance. This allows us to pray way beyond our own understanding and wisdom. This is perfect prayer from the perfect Holy Spirit, praying with and through you!

Once we have prayed in the Holy Spirit and discerned the mind of Christ we can pray in the understanding. Paul says to pray first in the Spirit then in the understanding 1 Cor 14:15. How often do we do it that way around?

CHAPTER NINE

THE THREE STAGES OF PRAYING IN THE HOLY SPIRIT

There are three phases, or stages, in releasing the prayer rivers of God using our prayer language to pray. The final stage is the point where the Spirit Himself pleads before God through us. At this stage He is leading the prayer and giving us the utterance.

I remember when I first experienced this level of prayer in the Spirit. I was lying on the floor in my lounge absolutely delighted I could pray in tongues. What a wonderful gift from God. I was listening to myself as I prayed and got more and more stirred up and vocal as I kept on speaking out. I grabbed a cushion off the sofa and buried my face in it because I was getting louder and louder. Suddenly I stopped completely because the thought occurred to me that I was just getting hysterical and being foolish. At the moment I stopped speaking out and was thinking this, loudly and clearly the Lord spoke to me and asked me a question, **"So you think this is foolish"?** He didn't need to say any more.

I knew it was God and immediately I remembered what Paul wrote in 1 Cor 2:14,

"But the natural, nonspiritual man does not accept or welcome or admit into his heart the gifts and teachings and revelations of the Spirit of God,

for they are folly (meaningless nonsense) to him and he is incapable of knowing them (of progressively recognizing, understanding, and becoming better acquainted with them) because they are spiritually discerned and estimated and appreciated." (Amplified Bible).

Immediately I understood both scripturally and experientially what it meant to pray in the Spirit. I replied to the Lord, "If this is being foolish (according to natural wisdom) I will be your fool!" And I have continued to this day being a fool for Christ praying in tongues in the Holy Spirit.

So back to the lounge, I continued praying in tongues again and even more vigorously. After a time the pressure to pray in tongues eased, then the power of God fell on me and I felt like I was being squeezed into the floor. The weight of God's glory was so strong I couldn't get up. What a wonderful moment in God!

So are you ready now to get into these realms of the Holy Spirit?

Let us go through the three stages of prayer in the Spirit now.

I am going to first look at the tabernacle in heaven as a picture of the three stages of prayer, and then look at what we do as we pray in tongues going through each stage of prayer.

Most of us have experienced the three stages of praise, to high praise, to worship in our meetings. This process is exactly the same. You come to a meeting and you do not really want to sing. As an act of your will you do. You then get to a place where it is easy to sing and you sense the energisation of the Holy Spirit. You move into "High Praises", and then after a time in that you move into worship before the throne. This is the same three stage pattern as that for prayer.

The Tabernacle is a picture of the Three stages of Prayer.

The tabernacle of Moses, a copy of the true tabernacle in heaven, is a type of our new lives in Christ. A triune structure which is a picture for us believers who are triune beings. I'll use this picture to show what happens when we pray in the Holy Spirit.

The outer court is the natural part of our lives. The Holy place is the place of our interaction with the Holy Spirit, who is God on the earth. The Holy of Holies is the place of God's throne-room where we are seated in Christ.

The tabernacle of Moses was an exact copy of the heavenly tabernacle which was made without human hands. It was in this heavenly tabernacle that Christ offered His blood. Heb 9:11–12.

So let us look at the earthly tabernacle of Moses to understand more about the tabernacle that is in heaven. The earthly tabernacle made by Moses had three sections. The first was the outer court. This was an area enclosed by a linen fence which was seven and a half feet high. If you were inside you could not see out, and if you were outside, you could not see in. The outer court was much larger than the covered sections which were also inside the linen fence.

For us new testament believers who have gone through the Door into new lives in Christ, this shows that we are hid in Christ. We are separated from the world.

There was only one gate into the outer court. Jesus is this gate. This is also a picture of Jesus Christ as the only way, because there is only one gate. John 10:9,

"I Am the Door; anyone who enters through Me will be saved."

When we the new covenant believer come into Christ we come through the gate, which is Jesus, into the outer court. We never leave this place by going back out the door or gate again because we are in Him and remain in Him. In the outer court there is no covering, it is open to normal light and the environment, so it is the place in Him where we can operate with the natural senses and abilities we have. This is a picture of our life in Christ as we live in the day to day.

How many of God's people never leave this place of natural living even though they are in Christ? I think far too many!

We live in the natural seen world and can operate in this world with our natural senses. However there is a higher call for every one of us. 1 Peter 2:5,

"We are called to be a royal priesthood to offer up spiritual sacrifices that are acceptable and pleasing to God through Jesus Christ."

We are urged to move beyond just an outer court experience with Christ, through the Holy Place into the very Holy of Holies. To do this we need first to approach the altar and laver. These are the only things in the outer court.

Rom 12:1 tells us that we are to present our bodies a living sacrifice to God which is our reasonable service. We choose to live for Christ. Yield our body to His service. We lay our lives down.

Rom 12:2 also tells us that we must be transformed by the renewing of our minds. This speaks of the washing of the water of the word (the laver is a picture of this). Why do we need to do this?

"so that you may prove what is the good and pleasing and perfect will of God for you."

How many people wonder what God's will is? Here is the answer to that need! Renew your mind! And then walk in the will of God for your life.

We need to make the above activities a lifestyle in our new life in Christ.

In a sense, when we choose to start praying in tongues, we normally start from this place of natural things. We choose as an act of our will to move into things of the Spirit. We start to build ourselves up praying in the Holy Spirit. As we do this and rise higher and higher as per Jude verse 20, the Spirit begins influencing us. As we persevere even more, He then starts to take us to the next place. This prayer activity can be seen as presenting your body a living sacrifice, and our mind has been renewed to the value in doing this.

The next place in Moses's tabernacle was a covered structure which was divided in two sections inside of it. Remember Moses's tabernacle was a copy of the tabernacle in heaven. Heb 8:2. Heb 9:11–12.

We then approach the Holy Place, the first part of this covered structure. Because the Holy Place is covered and enclosed, the only light in this place comes from the seven branched menora. Natural senses do not function in this place. This speaks of the Spirit of wisdom and revelation. There are two other pieces of furniture in the Holy Place. The table of showbread and the golden altar of incense. As we move into the things of the Spirit, we have to operate in the revelations of the Holy Spirit. Natural wisdom will have us fumbling around in the dark in this environment. So this is a place of connection to and inspiration from the Holy Spirit. The Light of God fills this place. This is a place of fellowship with God. The showbread speaks of fellowship. The Holy place is also a place of prayer, which is represented by the golden altar of incense. We looked at this prayer incense before the throne of God in Chapter Three.

Now as the Holy Spirit gives us the utterance and influences us more and more in our prayer in tongues, we move from the outer court in our prayer, into the place of influence and revelation of the Spirit. That is the Holy Place. The intensity and power of our prayer increases more and more as the Spirit empowers and energises us. More and more incense is released. We rise and fall in prayer waves and then the Holy Spirit begins to take us into the Holy of Holies.

Scripture tells us we have access to the Father by the Holy Spirit. Eph 2:18,

"For it is through Him that we both whether far off or near now have an introduction (access) by one Holy Spirit to the Father so that we are able to approach Him."

Scripture also tells us to come boldly into the Holy of Holies by the new and living way. Heb 10:19–23. So we go with and in the Holy Spirit into the Holy of Holies. God welcomes us into this place.

If we look at what the Holy Spirit does as we go into the 3rd stage of our prayer with God, He pleads before God. Rom 8:27,

"because the Spirit pleads ***before God*** *in behalf of the saints according to and in harmony with God's will."*

This pleading takes place in the heavenly Holy of Holies **before** God.

If you are "before" someone you are right in their presence.

This means, as we have access to the Father by the Spirit, we are right in the very Holy of Holies in heaven before God, as we work with the Holy Spirit in our intercession. Yet it is not our intercession but His intercession. That sounds like Paul in Gal 2:20 saying,

"I live, and yet not I, but Christ lives in me."

The Spirit pleads as "Advocate" before God on behalf of the saints. He is right in the throne room, He is in the Holy of Holies in heaven. And He has taken us there with Him.

So as we go through the 3 stages of "Praying with the Holy Spirit" we get to this place. We in the Holy Spirit, before the throne of God interceding for the saints.

As we finish the intercession we sense with awe God's Glory about us. We have been involved in God's work with Him. We have been successful in our petition at the heart of and involved in God's executive authority.

Not many people in this world get into the executive workings of earthly governments, let alone the working of God's eternal government. But we do! We petition Him in things pertaining to the saints and the earth.

I have noticed that when people in nations around the world get upset or have issues, they often carry placards in protest outside government buildings and might even throw rocks and things at government representatives. How much influence do they actually have doing this? Not as much as the people inside the cabinet sitting around the table with that nation's leaders.

We can enter right to the throne room of God. We the people of God don't carry placards around outside the throne room, but come right in boldly as the beloved sons we are, and present our petitions with and in the Holy Spirit right before the throne of God. Wow!

Then we have the right and authority to declare and release the will of God into the earth. Matt 16:19,

"I will give you the keys of the kingdom of heaven; and whatever you bind (declare to be improper and unlawful) on earth must be what is already bound in heaven; and whatever you loose (declare lawful) on earth must be what is already loosed in heaven." Amplified Bible.

Now I am going to look at the practical aspects of the three stages of prayer.

Stage one: Charging yourself up

I start to pray in my prayer language (other tongues). This is an act of my will and I can do it whenever I want to. This language is a gift from God to each of us. I start to "edify" myself as per 1 Cor 14:4. This means to build myself up, to charge myself, embolden myself, to rebuild, to repair myself. I like the analogy of the alternator in a motorcar edifying and charging up the battery as the motor runs. In the same way, as you pray in tongues you charge yourself up. Jude:20 says the same thing,

"But you, beloved, build yourselves up founded on your most holy faith make progress, rise like an edifice higher and higher praying in the Holy Spirit (other tongues)."

This is not a casual half-hearted activity, but a vigorous release of speaking in other tongues. Liken it to going for a walk every day to get yourself fit. If you stop after two minutes to smell the flowers and amble along slowly, your exercise will not get you breathing any harder and breaking into a sweat. You want to walk fast enough to get your second wind. You want to go beyond the first little discomfort. A walk like that is invigorating and once you have got into good physical condition, is refreshing. You are praying like this to get your second prayer wind.

Do not allow your mind to say, "Why are you doing this?" "This is a waste of time!" Remind yourself, "I am pushing through with this and will not stop until I have engaged with the Holy Spirit, prayed with Him and He has released me to stop."

Imagine if a singer never exercised their voice or a musician never learnt the scales and practised them. Set your mind before you start not to stop until something has been accomplished. I use the acronym P.U.S.H in my prayer life: Pray Until Something Happens.

Stage two: Your Second Wind

As you press through the first stage of your prayer and continue at it wholeheartedly, a pressure will begin to build in you, now you are starting to work. Increase your prayer tempo, put your weight into it. You could compare this phase to riding a bicycle up a hill. After a while as you continue working, speaking vigorously in tongues, it will feel like the hill you are climbing on your bicycle is levelling out. You will start to pick up more speed if you maintain your work rate. Then it gets exciting! You will feel you have started going downhill. Your prayer is being energised by the Holy Spirit, and you will be able to go on even more energetically. You have got your second wind in your prayer now. Sometimes at this point, it seems like a wind begins pushing you along from behind. An energy has started being released in you. You will sense you are not alone in what you are doing. You have started harmonising with the Holy

Spirit. Keep praying in tongues and lock your mind onto what you are doing, feeling and saying. The prayer is taking shape at this point.

This is good because what has happened now is that the Holy Spirit has energized you and is influencing your spirit in the prayer utterance more and more. Your spirit is now beginning to pray by the Holy Spirit within you. The Holy Spirit is starting to take hold of your prayer with you.

1 Cor 14:14 says,

"If I pray in an unknown tongue, my spirit by the Holy Spirit within me prays."

I often experience even more acceleration in my prayer tempo at this point, it is as if I am suddenly doing 60 miles an hour on my bicycle, going really fast and then sometimes I hit something, some sort of a barrier or resistance. If this happens I give it everything I have in me. I release all my energy and force into the prayer in tongues to get through what I have hit. It could take a few minutes or an hour or longer. This barrier could be a demonic stronghold or a mountain of some sort that is impeding my progress in God. Or blocking something He has promised me or I need.

Later as we pray in the Holy Spirit for others, these barriers are often something affecting our church, our city, our state or our nation. The prayer process we are discussing here is exactly the same when praying in the Holy Spirit for ourselves, other individuals or groups of people or even for nations.

I keep the prayer intensity up until I am through the resistance and cycling along nice and easily again in my prayer.

Every time you experience a resistance to your prayer in tongues then do what I just explained I do. Perhaps the Spirit has just lifted a heartache off of you, or has just brought a release into an area of your life.

Once the pressure is off keep bubbling away at an easy pace in your prayer tongue. Look again at this point to see what the Holy Spirit is doing. Listen to your tongue.

Try to identify whether your language and manner of speaking is still aggressive, or whether it is becoming a different type of prayer, a pleading, or it is moving into a birthing type of prayer. Or is your prayer building again in another wave similar to the one you have just finished.

If the tempo of your prayer is starting to increase again, go with the Holy Spirit. If it gets so fast that you cannot speak the words out fast enough start to sigh and groan. Your body will start to be affected. You might want to stamp, or clap, or raise your hands, or prostrate yourself. Go with the Holy Spirit.

Keep Going! **Release the prayer from your belly not your head.** It is like saying a loud "aaaaaahhhhhhh" from your stomach and not your head. The utterance we are releasing from our mouths is not mentally originated. It comes from our spirits by the Holy Spirit.

You are now moving into stage three of your prayer in the Holy Spirit.

We have now bypassed our intellect and understanding. This is an act of the highest humility and trust in God. Many people think the Holy Spirit is incapable of doing the job if they do not understand everything that is being prayed. This causes them not to use their prayer language very much, if at all. In 1 Cor 14:18 we see what Paul says about praying in the Spirit. He prays in tongues more than all the Corinthians put together. (Amplified Bible).

As the Holy Spirit takes a hold of our prayer together with us, **we greatly increase the influence of God by the Holy Spirit on our lives**. He is now praying with us. He is directly moving within us and giving us more and more utterance. The river of God is starting to flow from within us in greater and greater intensity! Now lock your attention onto what He is doing as you continue praying in and with the Holy Spirit. Look to see if you are getting a vision from Him, or look for understanding of what He is doing.

Do not stop praying in tongues at this point!

1 Cor 14:13 says that the person who prays in a tongue should pray for the power to interpret what he is saying. With your mind tell God you want to understand. If at first you do not understand, be patient, because He will give you understanding in time. Keep making a demand on Him for understanding as you continue praying in tongues.

Do you know you can pray a different prayer with your mind to that which you are praying with your spirit simultaneously?

Our minds and spirits can work independently from one another. For example I can drive my car and pray in tongues at the same time. This is why I tell you to lock your mind onto your tongues and concentrate on what the Holy Spirit is doing, especially when you are praying in tongues in a group. When I pray in tongues for a long time in my day to day activity, my mind does move onto other things. There is, however, always a part of me alert to my tongue so that if something starts changing in my tongue or I engage some resistance I immediately bring my attention back to my tongue and look to see or discern what is happening. I will pray in my mind, "Father, What is this?" as I continue speaking in tongues with my spirit.

What an amazing gift tongues is!

Stage Three: The Holy Spirit prays

When I get to this point I do not want to stop praying in the Holy Spirit. If I do, I feel frustrated. My spirit is now so aroused!

"thoroughly aroused by the Holy Spirit" 1 Cor 14:16. (Amplified Bible).

The Holy Spirit has now taken over the prayer as in Rom 8:26–27. He is either pleading or coming as a rushing stream flowing through and out of you. If He is pleading, this pleading is not begging. How can God beg God? This is the pleading of the Advocate in justification of what is asked. The case is perfectly presented in such a way that all petitions are granted from God's riches in Christ Jesus.

Advocate is another name of the Holy Spirit, John 16:7.

This can also be the beginning of birth pangs. The Holy Spirit is birthing something into this world.

The rushing stream of God that is mentioned in Isaiah 59:16 comes out of you. The Amplified bible translates this passage well,

"When the enemy shall come in like a flood, The Spirit of the Lord will raise a standard against him and put him to flight for the Spirit will come like a rushing stream which the breath of the Lord drives."

The river (the rushing stream) is flowing out of your innermost being driven by the breath of the Lord. John 7:38,

"He who believes in Me as the scripture has said, from his innermost being shall flow continuously springs and rivers of living water." (Amplified Bible).

Do not stop praying in and with the Holy Spirit yet.

Let the waves of prayer go through you. Paul calls these waves of prayer labour pangs or birth pangs, Gal 4:19. The waves of prayer are the rising in energy and intensity of the prayer. This then peaks or "climaxes" and is then followed by a quietening down time. The next wave of prayer will then begin to build up pressure to a peak and then quieten down again. As the prayer waves build and the intensity increases stay in step with the prayer rhythm of the Holy Spirit, getting more and more intense as the wave you are on peaks. As it ebbs, back off, but continue to let your prayer language bubble out of you and begin to build again as the Holy Spirit increases the intensity again to the next peak.

Stay in step with Him!

In my experience if I try to stay on a peak, when the wave of prayer I was on has finished, I will exhaust myself.

Another thing we need to watch for is that we are not too passive when the next prayer wave begins or we may get left behind. If the Holy Spirit increases the tempo and intensity of the next wave, stay with His rhythm and timing. Be strong in Him and in His mighty power. Draw your strength from Him, Eph 6:10.

I always think of Elijah in 1 Kings 18:43–44 sending his servant to look each time his prayer peaked and then ebbed, or to put it another way, each time a labour pang was completed. Finally by the end of the seventh wave the job was complete. There was a visible result.

Keep going! Do not stop praying with the Holy Spirit. The waves of prayer will be closer and closer together and will become more and more intense as the prayer in the Holy Spirit starts to reach a final climax or peak.

And then it is done!

An amazing peace and joy floods you. You sense the pleasure of God. You will want to stay in this atmosphere. You worship. It's a time of amazing intimacy with God.

Now you know first-hand why in Phil 4:7 the Word says,

"Present your prayers and petitions to God and the peace of God will guard your heart and guard your mind. It will garrison about you."

This peace is the title deed to the prayer you have just prayed.

If I said I was giving you £10,000 and you had the cheque in your hand you would go your way rejoicing. You would not give that cheque to someone else or destroy it because you got worried about how you would pay a £1000 bill you had. You would deposit it in your bank. That cheque is your guarantee that you will get that money. God's peace is His guarantee to you that your request has been granted. Don't let that guarantee be taken from you by going back into worry.

Rom 8:28 now applies to you,

"All things work to the good of those who love Him, God being a partner in their labour."

The Holy Spirit has been a partner with you in this labour!

If the pressure builds in me to get anxious about something I have already prayed through and got peace about, I go back to the Holy Spirit and water that thing with my prayer language in and with the Spirit, and move back into that place of peace.

So if we can go beyond our personal prayer language into the prayer language of the Holy Spirit (Intercessor), we partner with the Holy Spirit (God) to pray the perfect will of God for that situation. We allow the Holy Spirit to orchestrate and conduct the prayer until the job is done. How do we know when He is satisfied the job is done? He gives us the title deed to the prayer – that is the peace of God, Phil 4:6–7.

In this way we are to partner with God in our prayers! In childlike trust in Him and not having to work out everything with our limited minds we do this. We are partners and co-labourers with God. We come to Him boldly.

Our prayers are to be God breathed and Spirit prayed.

It is His Kingdom, and His perfect will that needs to be prayed every time we pray. We can achieve this by praying first in the Spirit and then in the understanding, the order that Paul puts it in 1 Cor 14:3–15.

In closing this section there is an amazing verse of scripture in Eph 3:20,

"Now to Him Who by the action of His mighty power that is at work in us is able to carry out His purpose and do super abundantly above all we ask or think or even imagine (infinitely beyond our highest prayers, desires, thoughts, hopes or dreams to Him be glory in the Church."

His mighty power at work in you is the Holy Spirit energizing and working in and through you in your prayers as you pray in the Holy Spirit.

See what happens when we do this consistently. You will be pursued and overtaken by the blessings God has already poured out on you. Eph 1:3.

Now put on the MP3 tracks and start to get on with practical aspects of "Praying with God".

These are available to download at: www.mobilisenow.com with the download of this book.

Track One will refresh and instruct in what you have just read.

Track Two will become your prayer track. This is your exercise track. This track will sensitize you to the way the Spirit flows and help you develop spiritual fitness. Learn to recognise the stages of praying in the Spirit with God by doing it.

CHAPTER TEN

CORPORATE PRAYER IN THE HOLY SPIRIT

Corporate prayer is extremely prominent in the Bible, and it should also be in our lives. It is a core part of our Christian experience. The descriptions of corporate prayer in the Bible paint a picture of prayer that is vital, explosive, powerful, extravagant, bold, successful, satisfying, life-changing, nation- changing. This is the opposite of some groups I have attended, where there is a dullness, and the meetings are boring, lifeless, and yawn inducing. Although there is absolutely no substitute for individual prayer, the results of group prayer can be more powerful and effective than praying alone. In this chapter we will look at some of the dynamics of effective group prayer.

Corporate prayers in the New Testament produced extremely powerful results.

In Acts 1:14, the power of the Holy Spirit was poured out in a prayer meeting which birthed the church. In its foundation stages the early church gathered daily in homes for corporate prayer, Acts 2:42. In Acts 4:23–31, the early church responded to challenges with corporate prayer. In Acts 6:4 the apostles considered it so vital to pray together that they appointed deacons to look after the widows and needy so that they could have more time for corporate prayer. In Acts 12, the church gathered to pray and the result was such a shaking that Peter was released from prison. In Acts 13:2–3 it was in a corporate prayer meeting that the apostles received direction to send Paul out on his missionary journeys.

If we want to see: 'deliverance' of the saints from 'prisons', direction for the people of God from the Lord, the sending out of people in power, answers to prayer and healing power manifesting in our lives, corporate prayer is the answer.

What brings life to these meetings is the leading, presence and power of the Holy Spirit and the reality of praying WITH God, as we have described in previous chapters.

Guidelines to praying in a group

Here are several guidelines and principles that can contribute to the success of a group meeting.

1. Vision and Focus

What do we want our prayer meeting to be like? We want meetings that are like those we see in the Bible, full of power, life and the Presence of God.

God centred. Most of our prayers are needs- focused, and centred around ourselves. We need to change our focus and transition to kingdom thinking. We can re-calibrate our thinking from 'sinner' to 'saint' and pray with executive and governmental power as representatives of God's kingdom on earth. We may need to make significant changes in our thinking and practice of prayer to do this.

We would like to see our prayer meetings filled with the Presence of God and power of God.

Acts 4:23–31 And when they had prayed, the place where they were assembled together was shaken; and they were all filled with the Holy Spirit, and they spoke the word of God with boldness.

The Presence of God and the power released resulted in visible transformation of people and situations. The Presence of God also resulted in edification and strengthening of those that prayed.

2. **Leadership**

I have led many meetings where people come in late without a clue of what it going on, and they then sit in the prayer meeting with their mouths wide open in shock. Many good potential intercessors have been put off praying in the Holy Spirit in corporate gatherings through lack of understanding or lack of instruction and good leadership. Sound leadership is necessary in a group in order to keep the group on task, to keep focus and to ensure the goal is achieved. Leadership is not dominance or control, but a vehicle for facilitating God's will.

A good leader will stay on track with the Holy Spirit. He or she will be sensitive to the Holy Spirit and be able to instruct the team in what the Holy Spirit is doing and complete whatever task He has given the group.

3. **Unity**

I looked up some information about the Amazon river a little while ago. The Amazon river is not the longest river in the world but in terms of water volume it is the biggest. Thousands of rivers flow into the Amazon river causing the power of its flow in flood to push fresh water hundreds of miles out to sea.

The power of the Amazon river is amazing but imagine if the rushing streams or rivers of God flowing out of small and large groups of Christians, all in unity, combined to become huge rushing torrents of Living water flowing through their neighbourhoods, counties and nations

These torrents would push all ungodliness and demonic activity out the way. Torrents of Living water would demolish strongholds and change atmospheres. The healing river that Ezekiel saw (Ezek 47:2–12) transformed the places it went. Ezekiel saw that the river flowed from the temple. We are now the temple of the Holy Spirit. In Rev 22:1 we see the river that flows from the throne of God and the Lamb. We are seated in Him in heavenly places. Could we be part of the source of this river? Of course we are! Rivers flow from the innermost being of those who believe in Him. John 7:38. The river of God will bring healing and deliverance to all in its path.

I have a dream to see all Christians everywhere in the world gathering together in unity in small and large groups to release their individual rivers of Living waters from their innermost beings as they pray in the Holy Spirit.

These rivers flowing together will combine into one large rushing torrent to cover peoples all over the earth in the Glory of God.

Habbakuk 2:14 tells us of an exciting time we are about to see,

"But the time is coming when the earth shall be filled with the knowledge of the Glory of the Lord as the waters cover the sea."

I see this happening very quickly if enough people are mobilised to pray in the Spirit. We can do this in our time. We can start doing this today in small groups everywhere. Get to learn teamwork as the size of the prayer group grows. Keep a prayer journal and it will soon be obvious what a huge impact your prayers are making. I believe this mobilisation of prayer in the Spirit will usher in to full manifestation the last great move of God that we are already sensing.

Get a friend to begin with, and pray along with the prayer track available at www.mobilisenow.com. This will teach you how to pray in the Spirit and make you sensitive to the rhythms of the Holy Spirit before coming to a "praying with God" prayer meeting.

Everyone who comes to these prayer meetings should be equipped through teaching or by listening to the mp3 teaching and then praying a long with the second mp3.

Alternatively someone must explain to everyone what is going to happen before the meeting is started. I would recommend that everyone who wants to attend a "Praying with God" corporate prayer meeting should have listened to the two MP3 tracks, read the book, and have practised praying along with the mp3 and got familiar with the ways of the Spirit in prayer before going to the corporate prayer meetings.

Practicalities of the meetings.

1. The leader or facilitator should start the prayer meeting by saying something like the following:

   We are going to pray corporately in tongues, every one of us together at the same time.

   Every one of us will break the sound barrier. This is not silent prayer. The aim is not to pray what we think or need right now but to yield ourselves to Him as one person, to pray what The Holy Spirit leads us to pray. We don't stop until He is finished. Then we can change the type of prayer we continue the meeting with.

   We are not singing, watching, doing our own thing. This is like push-starting a car! The momentum comes more easily if everyone pushes simultaneously. The rivers must all flow to get the force behind the rushing river (like the Amazon river, and the river that Ezekiel saw or the river in the book of Revelations).

One person holding back diminishes what we can achieve because the pressure we are exerting in the spiritual realm is less.

2. Invite the Holy Spirit to pray with you. Tell Him you want to yield your spirit, mind, emotions and body to Him to pray anything He wants to pray, and ask Him to help you stay in step with Him. Each time He takes you deeper into the river go with Him. We are going to get to the place where His river carries us completely. Don't stop at your ankles, or knees, or waist. Go right into the deep water and get into the current and get carried down the river by that current. Ezek 47:1–9.

3. Start to pray in tongues briskly like going for a fast walk. The whole group must stay together praying at the same intensity and speed. Do not let some sing or wail or do their own thing. Keep everyone together. Then you will not get weird behaviour hijacking the prayer meeting.

4. Move into the place of your second wind. The place where the Holy Spirit starts to energise you. If people in the group are getting left behind get behind them in the Spirit and push them along. It might be necessary if this doesn't get them working properly to stop the prayer and encourage them to keep up. If anyone holds back the others have to work harder so the whole group is affected by this. Imagine your group is pushing a car up a hill, you need everyone present to put their weight into it.

5. Pray from your bellies not your minds. Consciously release the river of prayer.

6. Listen to your tongue. The words, the weight behind them and their tone. Empathise with your tongue, let yourself go with it (trust the Holy Spirit). Start to focus your mind on what you are doing. Ask God what's going on. Ask God for pictures and visions as you pray. Maybe God will take you somewhere as you pray. In Col 2:5 (Paul is with

them in spirit) or Rev 1:10 and Rev 4:1, John was in the Spirit when this happened.

7. Go with the flow and rhythms of the Spirit. Up and down. Like the eagle on the updrafts and winds. Rise higher and higher on your eagle wings. Discern as you change gear in the Spirit.

   Listen to the prayer language and prayer tempo of those around you. If someone starts to get into something get everyone to run behind them and push. (You will hear a change in their pitch and a change in their prayer intensity).

8. Persevere! Continue! Actively push. If nothing seems to be happening push harder. Smith Wigglesworth said, "If the Spirit doesn't move me I move the Spirit."

9. Take hold of the prayer. Partner with the Holy Spirit.

10. Work as a team. Again if one gets into something everyone must run in behind them. Roman soldiers locked their shields together and advanced with a wall of steel all around them.

    I like the picture of a rugby team doing rolling mauls. One player has the ball and everyone gets behind him to push him forward. Those who fall over or off the side of the maul run around to the back of the maul to put their weight into the push again. We want to take every person into breakthrough in this prayer. If someone gets through and others haven't, that person must run back into the prayer push and get behind the others to push everyone through.

11. Be ready to give it everything you have got at the right time. That's when we pray as if someone is sitting with his finger on the button of nuclear devices aimed at our town and only our prayers can stop him pressing that button. The earnest, intense, heartfelt prayers of a righteous man avail much (James 5:16). Increase your intensity tenfold, and then double it again.

Your prayers are seeding and changing the atmosphere and releasing the breath of God in the situation you are praying into with the Holy Spirit. (Like the Amazon River whose thousands of tributaries flow together to push fresh water hundreds of miles out to sea). Our rivers of Living water flow together to be a rushing torrent which the breath of the Lord drives Isaiah 59:16. (Amplified Bible).

The very rivers we release from our innermost being, becomes the power that carries us along. If the river gets fast or we go through a bumpy section do not try to get out. We will always end up in a tranquil place in Him if we go all the way and complete the prayer task we have been partnering with the Holy Spirit in.

When the prayer has climaxed slow down to a place of rest. Enjoy the presence of the Father and Son in the Spirit, Who will be all over you.

Often when I have been in prayer meetings as we reach this rest and intimacy with God, He asks us to ask Him for anything we want and He delights to give it to us. He delights in the fact you have laid your life down for what the Spirit has wanted to pray for others, or for pushing aside strongholds He wanted moved. Personal petition is so easy at this time and so quickly dealt with so you can continue to fellowship with the Father and Son and Holy Spirit.

In my opinion prayer meetings like this are the best of all the Church meetings you can ever experience as a Christian.

"The Kingdom of God is righteousness peace and joy in the Holy Spirit."

CHAPTER ELEVEN

A CALL FOR ACTION

Please do not just read this book and do nothing with what you have read. Every one of us can pray. Get a friend or two together, put on the 15 minute teaching on track One of the two MP3's available to facilitate "Praying With God". When you have understanding of what this is about, put on track Two and begin to pray along and learn and practice praying with God. Go deeper and deeper in this until you are regularly travailing in the Holy Spirit.

As more and more of us do this we will see what Habakkuk prophesied in Habakkuk 2:14 beginning to happen,

"But the time is coming when the earth shall be filled with the knowledge of the glory of the Lord as the waters cover the sea."

I believe this time has come and now we need to do something about this scripture.

Prophetically the "sea" in the above quotation from Habakkuk represents the peoples or nations of the earth. So as we the people of God release the Living waters and the sounds of heaven from within us, praying in the Holy Spirit, the rivers flowing from within us will cover the peoples of the earth. If enough of us mobilise and pray in the Spirit with continued heartfelt prayer, dynamic power will be released. (James 5:16). This is how I believe this promised last days outpouring which has begun, will gather momentum!

This will be an outpouring begun, sustained and increased in measure by the church universal mobilising, and by every saint everywhere stepping up and getting involved.

Revival has a sound. Sound has an effect on us. Upbeat music can energise us. Imagine scary movies without the music and sound at times of tension. Most of the tension would never be created. I still remember the music from Jaws the movie about the shark. I used to hear it in my head each time I went surfing.

Sound is also a weapon. The police are using sound to disperse rioters. These devices are called sonic cannons. Apparently when operated, sonic cannons cause pain in the people within their range, and this causes them to run away.

The weapons of our warfare also have a sound. We have discussed how Balem could not curse Israel because the shout of the Lord was in their midst. Num 23:21.

Breakthrough has a sound. Victory has a sound. It was a sound that brought down the walls of Jericho. We need the sound of breakthrough in our lives. I have heard many Christians talking about their need for a breakthrough in their lives. This has prompted me to search this out. The Lord spoke to me and said, "Breakthrough has a sound!" We need to agree with this sound. The birthing of new things in the kingdom of God has a sound.

Jesus prayed with, "loud crying and tears" in the days of His flesh. Heb 5:7. That was a sound.

The Amplified Bible says in Matt 18:19, *"Again I tell you, if two of you on earth agree, (harmonize together, make a symphony together) about whatever (anything and everything) they may ask, it will be done for them by My Father in heaven."*

Thayer's Greek Lexicon defines "agree together" in Matt 18:19 as: *to sound together, be in accord together as musical instruments, to harmonize.*

So we need to harmonize with the sounds of breakthrough and travail in the heavenlies. We will then see The Kingdom manifest on the earth in our lives. What does this mean in plain words? You can either stir yourself in the Spirit and get to a place where you make the sounds of breakthrough and travail harmonising with the Holy Spirit by yourself, or get to a corporate meeting where this happens. Another way to do this is to get a recording of the "Breakthrough or Travailing" sound, put it on quite loud in your house or car, or wherever you are, and harmonize with it. In other words join in with the sound the recording releases. (Break the sound barrier with your own voice). The sound of "Breakthrough"carries the power for the "Breakthrough". The sound of Travail carries the power to birth new things, new saints, and to form Christ in you and others. Gal 4:19.

The Words Jesus spoke were sound. The words of God spoken out your mouth are sound!

Go to www.mobilisenow.com for a free download. Hover your mouse over "Media", go down the list in the drop down to the Battle in Wales, right click and download. Let the sound of Breakthrough fill your house. Harmonise with it and agree with it. Below that sound is the sound of Travail, do the same with that.

Every saint needs to be releasing these sounds. I believe the sound coming from many saints together, praying in the Holy Spirit, is the voice of many waters. Jesus speaks with the voice of many waters. He speaks through us.

The One who speaks with the voice of many waters, Jesus, wants to speak from within every one of you to cover the peoples of the earth in His glory. Why does He speak with the voice of many waters? The answer is because He speaks through the rivers of Living water that flow out from every "son of God" who has mobilised the flow of these rivers in their lives.

Ezek 43:2, *"And, behold, the Glory of the God of Israel came from the way of the east and His voice was like the noise of many waters and the earth shined with His Glory."*

Rev 1:15, *"And His feet like unto fine brass, as if they burned in a furnace; and His voice as the sound of many waters."*

Father Nash working alone at times, and at other times with only two or three others, was able to change atmospheres in cities in just a few weeks. What could we the body of Christ do if many thousands of us prayed travailing prayers consistently all over the world for the next few months or years.

The Living waters will cover the peoples of the earth. With this will be the increase in understanding of the Glory of God. How He works, what He says, and how to be fully connected and fruitful in Him.

We will get to know the Glory of the Lord, that is The Spirit of Glory.

The violent take the Kingdom by force. Let us be violent, change our routines and schedules and make time to do this.

We need to get into small groups in every city in every place in the world and begin to let the rivers flow from out of our innermost beings by praying in groups in the Holy Spirit wherever we are.

Will you be violent and do this?

You are in Him, He's in you. The Father is in you and the Spirit is in you. You are seated in Him. You have the mind of Christ. Resurrection power is in you! Eph 1:17–19.

What more do you need God to do for you? You have all you need to get started.

Get mobilised and you will see the Kingdom of God manifest in your life, your family, your town your city and your nation if small groups everywhere get together to pray regularly in the Spirit.

We must stop crying out to God to do something. We must do something! Now!

Invest in the advancement of the Kingdom and see how your lives will be fruitful and blessed. Every one of you can do something, you are not helpless or powerless. Let the rivers of Living water flow from your innermost beings by praying in the Spirit. Many rivers flowing together will cause the floods of the Spirit we are all longing for. Let us release the Amazon river of the Lord to flood the earth.

Get the "Praying with God" bundle from the MobiliseNow website and get started.

Rom 8:28 New [illegible]

All things work for the good of those who [illegible] God being a partner in their labour.

The Holy Spirit has been a partner with you in this labour [illegible]

If the pressure builds in me to get anxious about something I have already prayed through and got peace about, I go back to the Holy Spirit and water that thing with my prayer language in and with the Spirit and move back into that place of peace.

So if we can go beyond our personal prayer language into the prayer language of the Holy Spirit (intercessor), we partner with the Holy Spirit (God) to pray the perfect will of God for that situation. We allow the Holy Spirit to orchestrate and conduct the prayer until the job is done. How do we know when He is satisfied the job is done? He gives us the title deed to the prayer – that is the peace of God. Phil 4:6-7.

In this way we are to partner with God in our prayers in childlike trust in Him and not having to work out everything with our limited minds as we do this. We are partners and co-labourers with God. We come to Him boldly.

Our prayers are to be God breathed and Spirit prayed.

It is His kingdom and His perfect will that needs to be prayed every time we pray. We can achieve this by praying first in the Spirit and then in the understanding, the order that Paul puts it in 1 Cor 14:15.

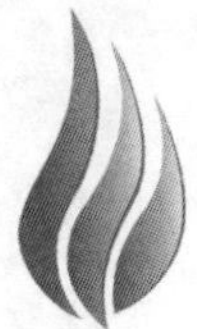

CHAPTER TWELVE

GET THE MESSAGE OUT

Thank you for reading this book. Please help me to get these prayer tools into more people's hands. Be part of mobilising the people of God by telling them about these tools, the MobiliseNow website and most of all your testimony of what is happening to you as you "Pray With God".

I have tried to give understanding and instruction in what "Praying with God" is about concisely in this book. I hope each one who has read this book will continue with their own study in areas I have not fully unpacked. My prayer is that you all experience things I have written about and that God will take you all into your own adventures with Him.

Persevere in prayer! Persevere in prayer! Persevere in prayer! Never ever ever give up!

Remember we have to lay aside our personal agendas, and many things we have learned up to now, for the birthing of the things God is bringing into being at this time. Trust Him to lead you as you pray for yourself and others. Be a partner with God in prayer projects in this the new season we have already entered into.

Blessings!

John and Heather Alcock

Founders of Mobilisenow

www.mobilisenow.com